Partner Selling

Produce Extraordinary Sales Results Without Hard-Sell Tactics

Bob Frare

Adams Media Corporation
Holbrook, Massachusetts

Published by
Adams Media Corporation
260 Center Street, Holbrook, MA 02343. U.S.A.
www.adamsmedia.com

ISBN: 1-58062-290-9

Printed in Canada.

J I H G F E D C B A

Library of Congress Cataloging-in-Publication Data
Frare, Robert E.
Partner selling : produce extraordinary sales results without hard-sell tactics / by Robert E. Frare.
p. cm.
Includes index.
ISBN 1-58062-290-9
1. Selling. I. Title.
HF5438.25 .F72 2000
99-055559

This publication is designed to provide accurate and authoritative information with regard to the subject matter covered. It is sold with the understanding that the publisher is not engaged in rendering legal, accounting, or other professional advice. If legal advice or other expert assistance is required, the services of a competent professional person should be sought.
— From a *Declaration of Principles* jointly adopted by a Committee of the American Bar Association and a Committee of Publishers and Associations

This book is available at quantity discounts for bulk purchases.
For information, call 1-800-872-5627.

A Note about the Term "Client"

Throughout this book, I have used the term client generically to mean everyone with whom you do business: external customers, internal customers, organization members, patients, and so on.

Dedications

To my parents, Ed and Peggy Frare, for creating an environment that nourished self-esteem, a desire to reach for the stars, and the perseverance to weather any storm.

And to my daughter Jaime—for being you.

TABLE OF

Contents

Acknowledgments

Many people encouraged me to write this book and aided immeasurably in its completion. Among them I would like to express my special appreciation to:

All the people who have attended my seminars over the years.

Dale Carnegie and Associates, who first exposed me to the world of training, self-development, and public speaking that I still find fascinating twenty years later.

Ron Willingham, Chairman of Integrity Systems, Inc., and all the outstanding people connected with that organization.

All my friends and colleagues at the National Speakers Association.

My brother Jerry Frare; Laurie Field, whose many talents include editing; Mark Fitzgerald; Nicole and Tim Van Epps; George Osley; Herman Sorin; Ken Rawley; Jim DeBerry; Donna Fisher; Jeff Levine; and John McCarty, whose contribution to this book exemplifies "partnering" in its purest form. I thank you!

—Bob Frare

INTRODUCTION

Partnering: The Key to Survival in the Twenty-First Century

"The supplier who doesn't become a business partner and come to grips with the new buyer-seller environment is bound to fail."

Recently, my friend Gene, who is president of a statewide association, called looking for a recommendation for a financial speaker to address his state meeting.

I gave him two prospects. He talked to both before making a decision.

The first speaker he contacted asked a lot of questions about Gene's organization, the personal and professional makeup of its membership, the specific outcome Gene wanted to achieve, and so on, to determine if there was a good matchup.

The second speaker Gene called asked no questions.

After Gene gave him a brief, general description of what he was looking for, the second speaker launched into a long-winded monologue about how great a speaker he was and what he thought he could do for Gene's organization. He was very price-focused and attempted to close Gene right away.

Gene told me later that he came away from the conversation with the first speaker with a very positive feeling.

Unable to get a word in edgewise with the second speaker, he came away not feeling very good—because there had been no attempt at partnership.

Guess who got the job?

In fact, not only did my friend go with the first speaker he called, but they are now talking about how this speaker can become a consultant to many of the organization's client companies.

The speaker's opportunity grew from a small one to one with much larger potential, all by asking a few need-development questions, by listening as well as talking, in order to determine if a win-win outcome was possible for both parties.

Changing Times

The nature of the client-supplier relationship has changed radically. Because of competition, changing loyalties, commoditization, and other factors, today's clients insist on getting the most for the time and money they spend.

Today's clients want to deal with fewer suppliers, and they expect those suppliers to do more for them on a consistent basis.

Their concerns are specific and extend beyond the transaction itself. They do not want to be treated as targets by sales people whose only interest is the bottom line. Their attitude translates to a desire to feel that they are *understood as individuals*—and that principled sales people will meet even the subtlest of their needs.[1]

With so many options available to them, clients no longer have to "take what they can get."

And they don't!

Restoring Your Competitive Edge

Just a few years ago, it wasn't possible to buy a high-ticket item like a computer from anyone but the manufacturer. Today, the computer industry has been commoditized. We can buy a computer from a mail order catalog, over the Internet, or from any one of a hundred sources.

The result? The consumer's decision whether to go with one computer supplier or another boils down to one key factor—price. Many times, price is the *only* factor.

There are so many outlets available today for just about any product or service that the danger of commoditization is starkly real—in any business and in any industry.

The commoditization of a product or service can be good for the client because it can lead to lower prices.

It is *not good* for the manufacturer making the product or the company offering the service, because it narrows the

[1] Ron Willingham, president of Integrity Systems, Inc., has been a pioneer in addressing this critical sea change in the buyer-seller relationship, which he sees as applying across the board, from retail customers to the clients of the largest industrial grants.

opportunities available for gaining a competitive edge. It makes price *all-important* by removing you, the expert, from the scenario—short-circuiting your ability and opportunity to provide the client with value. This must be avoided at all costs!

Partnering is the means by which you can *de-commoditize* your product or service and refocus your client on a more important target: *the value he or she is getting by buying from you rather than someone else.*

Partnering can restore your competitive edge.

Partner Selling focuses on what each party, the seller *and* the buyer, seeks to accomplish over the long term, and on how to develop a relationship that can help both parties achieve their mutual goals.

The process boils down to gathering information from the client—rather than the traditional approach of dumping a lot of, "Lemme tell ya what I can do for you" on him or her to try to rush a short-term sale.

It involves entering into a creative, nontraditional relationship with the client in order to succeed in today's highly competitive and volatile marketplace.

Partner Selling will show you, step-by-step, how to achieve this relationship with clients, prospects, and anyone else with whom you desire a win-win outcome.

CHAPTER ONE

Partner Selling: The Key to Successful Partnering

"The difference between success and failure is directly related to the relationship created and developed with clients."

It's been my experience, after working with hundreds of companies and thousands of sales people over the past twenty years, that the difference between success and failure is directly related to the relationship created and developed with clients.

The tricky, manipulative selling techniques of the past, such as "close early and close often," or "the sale begins when the client says no," and so on, no longer work—and turn everyone off, clients and sales people alike.

All things being equal—good quality products, sound business integrity, unbeatable service—only understanding how your prospect or client will gain value from doing business with you will give you the competitive edge you need today.

This is why Partner Selling goes beyond making the transaction. It offers a method for increasing your effectiveness by having a stake in your client's success.

It is based on a philosophy that says a good sale is one where both the buyer and the seller benefit, or a "win-win."

One example of how to successfully employ this philosophy is given by Robbie Krohl—brother and brother-in-law to Chris and Michelle Asterino of Phoenix, the two best hosts in the entire state of Arizona. Robbie sells high-end advertising for a specialty publication that trumpets the state's virtues.

Robbie does a lot of prospecting and makes mostly direct cold calls on potential customers. He has a finite amount of time to make his case with these busy people and complete the sales process. Typically, he gets one meeting, or just one shot, to accomplish this goal. As a result, he spends most of the meeting trying to find out what his prospects specifically want their advertising dollars to achieve, and building trust and rapport. He does this by getting the customer to do most of the talking. If he sees the potential for a win-win fit between the customer's specific needs and what he has to sell, he quickly proceeds to demonstrate how positioning their ads in his publication will meet those needs.

Robbie closes a high percentage of thc people he calls on because of his Partner Selling approach. In fact, he says that his relationship with his customers typically becomes so strong that they often seek his advice on how to get the most from their other advertising dollars. Robbie's customers see him bringing more value to the table than his product alone traditionally delivers, since he gladly and eagerly "gives away" his consulting advice. He sees it as part of the value, the win-win potential that he brings to the relationship.

Traditional versus Partner Selling

Several years ago I was asked to present a sales training program to an auto company with 84 dealerships in the New England area.

I wanted to be prepared, so I invested some time beforehand visiting six of their dealerships to see for myself how their people sold, what strategies and methods they were currently using, and so on. I parked my car in front of the showroom, entered the dealership, and behaved like a customer waiting to be approached.

What happened next in each of my six visits was fascinating.

If I happened to be standing next to the XY model when the sales person approached me, I got the routine XY pitch.

If I was looking at the XZ model, I got the routine XZ pitch I'm sure had been given to twenty clients before me and would be given to the twenty after me.

In each case, the sales person focused on giving me all the product information I could possibly absorb and totally neglected my needs as an individual. It was simply assumed that just because I was standing next to, or looking at, that model, *it* was the car I wanted, needed, and should have, regardless of whether it best suited my requirements, which went unexplored.

These sales people made me feel invisible.

This method of selling, taught in sales classes and training sessions for the past fifty years, is called Traditional Selling.

It teaches sales people to "product dump," to do most of the talking and to close hard, early, and often.

Traditional selling programs teach very manipulative tactics designed to get prospects to buy, whether the product is right for them or not.

This is no longer viable in today's world where clients require—indeed *demand*—more from the selling process than hearing about all the bells and whistles.

I believe this method causes clients to mistrust sales people and results in lost sales.

The ineffectiveness of traditional selling methods has become even more obvious with the emergence of so many "nontraditional sales" people in today's labor force.

These are people who never viewed themselves as sales people, either by personality or choice, but who have suddenly been thrust into a situation where they must become sales people by changes in their industry, company, or job.

Traditional selling techniques are alien, even anathema, to them. These tactics go against their grain.

Such methods run contrary to how they are accustomed to treating people, and how they want to be treated themselves.

Forced into a traditional selling mode, they feel like the proverbial square peg inserted into a round hole. They feel resentful, are almost inevitably unsuccessful, and burn out fast.

Traditional selling methods prompt people to adopt a negative attitude about selling. If such a view remains, sales will always be low.

Partner Selling shows them a way to sell which can be consistent with their personality and values.

In traditional selling, the largest block of time is spent negotiating and closing. In other words, make assumptions, offer generalizations, close hard. If that doesn't work—keep negotiating and close again.

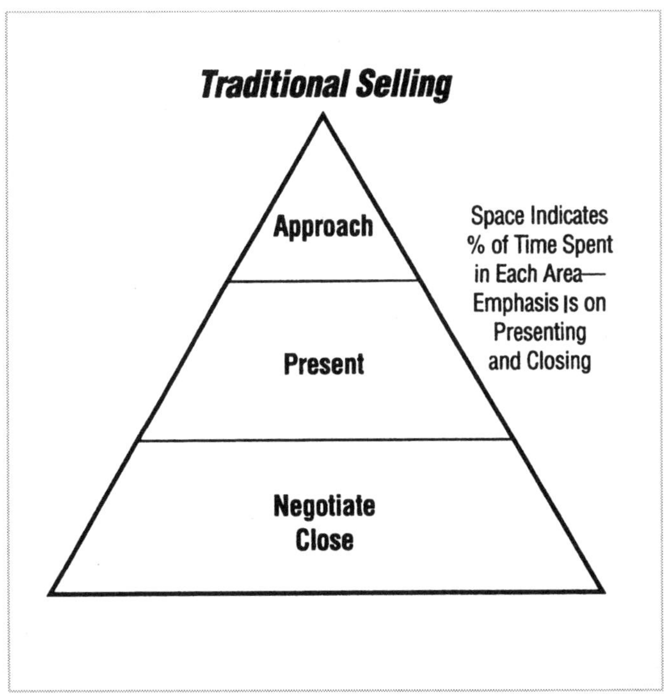

In Partner Selling, the process is reversed. No assumptions are made.

The largest block of time is now spent building rapport with the client in order to discover their needs and wants.

Product presentation takes up the next largest block of time.

The smallest block, the smallest focus, is for negotiating and opening a relationship.

Why?

Because if you spend the majority of your time finding out what the client's needs, problems, and concerns are, establishing a relationship, building a level of trust, gaining an understanding of whether there is or isn't a match between

Partner Selling

what the client's goals and requirements are and what you have to sell, then negotiation and opening the relationship will fall quickly and naturally into place.

People who sell for a living prefer the Partner Selling approach because it removes stress from the selling process.

It makes them feel good about what they're doing.

Clients like it, too, and as a result, respond more positively to the sales person.

By finding out if there is a genuine sales opportunity before moving forward with the process, the sales person is able to move forward with confidence and conviction.

He or she *believes*, "What I am offering you, the client, is really what you need to achieve your goals."

A few weeks ago, I was returning from a speaking engagement trip in a rented car. I had driven about four hours in a downpour.

I pulled into the rental place just as it was closing and stepped from the car under a canopy to get out of the teeming rain. I was stretching. My back hurt. I was tired, and just wanted to get home.

Suddenly, the man who parks the cars—the lowest person organizationally in the company—came walking out of the garage and approached me.

He smiled and said, "You're Bob Frare, aren't you?"

I nodded. Then he said, "You rent a lot of cars from us, don't you?" I nodded again. And he said, "I just wanted to let you know that we appreciate your business."

Well, I immediately perked up. I didn't feel tired or irritable anymore because he made me feel *valued*!

He could have been in a different mood very easily. He could have been surly or upset about having to go out into the rain. (Maybe he was. But he didn't let it show.) He took the time to make me feel like he cared and was happy that I was doing business there.

He made no assumptions. Offered no generalizations. Rather he spent the bulk of his time building trust and rapport.

He partnered with me.

Now, I know for a fact that this particular car rental company is very client-oriented. You're always escorted to your car when you rent. They walk you through every step of the car's operation. The company does all the right things to be client-friendly. From the way you're treated, you feel it immediately, which is why I continue to do business with this company.

But the important lesson here is not that the company has this philosophy, but that even the lowest person in the organizational ladder *practices* it.

Jon Denney, President of Camelot Legal Copy and my "printing partner," provides volume copying, color copying, printing, document imaging, and duplicating services. He recounts the following anecdote about how his firm put this philosophy into practice:

"It was 9:15 on a Wednesday morning. Ken Fell, Senior Vice President of Synquest (a worldwide software developer), had a flight scheduled for 12:36 P.M. that same day. Synquest's new product release manual had just been completed, and Ken needed fifty-three copies of this hefty manual to take with him on the flight for a meeting with his corporate senior management team, which was being flown to the same destination from locations all around the world. If these copies were not completed prior to his flight, the meeting would be seriously compromised, and the trip a big waste of everyone's time and Synquest's money.

"There was no way Ken's firm could produce the required number of copies itself in time, so he called on us. Given the size of the project and the fast turnaround, we realized doing so would be an amazing feat even for us to accomplish! But we did not look at this challenge as just a straight, fast turnaround 'copying job.' Rather we saw it as an opportunity to show Ken how we really go to bat for our customers by offering *all* the help they need when that help is needed the most.

"We mobilized the entire Camelot production staff into action, even pulling in our entire sales force and administrative personnel to assist. As the project neared completion, we realized there would not be sufficient time to deliver all the copies to Ken's office and still give him enough time to make his plane. So, we called him with a 'heads-up,' got his flight number, and told him we'd meet him at the gate. The next problem we faced was what to put all the copies in so that Ken would be able to carry them easily. A traditional copy box wouldn't do. We remembered an old suitcase we'd found in the office when we moved in, but for some reason had never gotten around to tossing, and quickly emptied it.

"As fate would have it, all fifty-three copies fit inside. We pulled up to the airport at 12:32. I grabbed the suitcase and ran to the gate where Ken was waiting, all the other passengers having already boarded the plane. I told him the copies were in the suitcase, handed it to him saying he needn't return it to us, wished him a safe flight, and off he went, pleased as punch.

"Sure we delivered the job on time, but the real value we provided was our *attitude.* The suitcase, the mad dash to the airport . . . those were *added value services.* We took on the project with the same sense of urgency the customer had. We viewed his problem as *our* problem. We conveyed the message that solving it was just as important to us as it was to him. And consistently went above and beyond to prove it."

The lesson this demonstrates is clear. As a process, Partner Selling must be driven from the top down. But it functions from the bottom up. If the company's philosophy is client-focused, but the frontline troops behave otherwise, the philosophy is useless.

Partner Selling must be fully supported by management in order to exist.

But to take root, it must be reinforced within the company on a continuing and consistent basis through training at every level.

Points to Remember:

- A good sale benefits buyer *and* seller.
- How you sell should be consistent with your personality and values.
- A win-win opportunity fuels the conviction to move forward.
- Build trust and rapport, understand the client's needs, and the sale will fall into place.

CHAPTER TWO

The Three Areas of Selling Competency

"Product knowledge alone does not make sales."

Numerous studies have been made over the years to determine what is essential to become an effective sales person.

These studies reveal three areas of selling competency, each of which must be fully mastered for the sales person to be successful:

- Product knowledge
- Selling skills
- Attitude

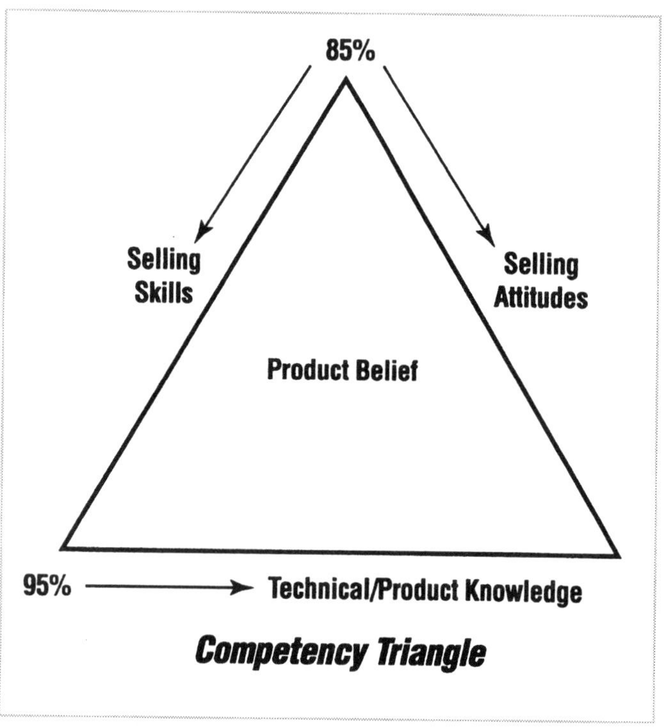

Competency Triangle

Product Knowledge

Product knowledge provides a platform on which to build your selling proficiency.

It is the essential information a sales person must have to be able to sell a particular product or service.

For most sales professionals, product knowledge becomes an ongoing flow of information—especially in high tech industries where changes are rapid and the need to stay current is critical.

As much as 95 percent of a sales person's education and training is spent gaining more product knowledge.

The problem is that product knowledge alone does not make sales.

Concentrating on product knowledge to the exclusion of all else tends to throw the sales person out of balance. Sales people become so loaded down with technical expertise and the jargon that comes with it that, at best, they wind up confusing the client. At worst, they wind up turning the client off. They aren't able to "read the client." As a result, they fail to present the product information in a way that will make the client respond to it most favorably. Inevitably, they are both amazed and frustrated when they don't complete the sale.

Product knowledge is not the same as product belief.

Product belief, unlike product knowledge, significantly affects a sales person's performance. It stems from a firm conviction that the product or service will do what the sales person says it will do, that the company will back up the product or service, and that a solid match exists between the product or service and the client/prospect's needs.

As I write this, I am about to conduct a sales training program for a large manufacturer of outdoor power equipment in Orlando, Florida.

The manufacturer has invited me to address its independent dealers from across the country, who have come to view the company's latest product line.

In reviewing the agenda, I am not at all surprised to see that I am the only speaker who will be addressing a subject other than product.

This scenario is not unusual.

Product knowledge is generally what companies focus on because it's what they're proficient in. But the end-user, the client, needs *more* than product information to enter into a buying relationship.

Studies show, in fact, that product knowledge accounts for just 15 percent of the reason why a sale is made.

What seals the deal is the sales person's proficiency in the remaining two, all too often neglected, areas of selling competency.

Selling Skills

Skills are defined as something demonstrable, a proficiency others can see.

In 1994, I witnessed the young tennis star Andre Agassi play an exhibition match with the aging John McEnroe. It was played the day after Agassi had won the title of the best tennis player in the world at the U.S. Open. His skill level was so high that he toyed with McEnroe throughout the match simply to make it interesting for himself and the spectator, finishing him off only when he was ready.

Shortly after the exhibition was played, I saw a *60 Minutes* interview in which Agassi revealed that when someone plays him well, it makes him feel he can lift his game to the next level and overpower his opponent. That statement shows extreme confidence in the skill area.

Sales people need to have the same kind of confidence in their own selling skills.

These skills include:

- Goal setting
- Prospecting
- Time and territory management
- Rapport building
- Asking questions
- Listening
- Translating value
- Negotiating
- Opening relationship
- Discipline to work alone
- Follow-up
- Presentation skills

These skills aren't always natural—sometimes they have to be learned in response to new or more challenging circumstances. For example, my daughter Jaime, while in the seventh grade, got a poor report card. She had received straight As all her life. Now, suddenly, she was getting Cs and Ds.

I asked her about this, and she said she had "no clue" why this was happening. Her mother and I immediately called for a conference at Jaime's school to diagnose the problem.

Her teachers unanimously agreed that Jaime was a very bright student, who had no problem absorbing the curriculum. In other words, her product knowledge was high. She was sociable and *liked* learning, so the problem was not attitude.

The cause of her poor grades lay elsewhere.

Jaime simply wasn't getting her assignments in on time.

Seventh grade is a big change for a student. Jaime was no longer in one class with one teacher, but now had to deal with six, each in a different subject.

For the first time in her life, she had to be organized in a way she'd never had to be before. She simply didn't have the skills.

So, with some resistance from my daughter, I worked with her to develop her organizational skills; she got her assignments in on time, and her grades have markedly improved.

When developed and mastered, these skills will lead the sales person to the next level of selling competency and result in a prosperous career.

Attitude

Our skills affect our attitude and vice-versa.

In other words, if I develop a greater level of skill at something, I am going to feel better about doing it.

We also communicate our attitudes to other people. Attitude determines what we think of a person—and makes us decide whether we want that person as a client or not.

Many instructors in the self-development field believe attitude is the single most important factor in determining a sales person's success or failure.

I havc a golfing partner named Frank who regularly shoots a score of around 82, 83. One day, he shot 75, a six-stroke improvement over his usual score, and won the match between us. As I gave him some money and we walked off the eighteenth green, he looked at me with a smile and said, “Let’s go again!”

I smiled back and said, “No thanks.”

Most of the time, eighteen holes are enough for Frank. But that day, he was so confident in his skill level that his attitude was transformed; he was at his best. Happily for me he has since “recovered” from this major improvement.

POINTS TO REMEMBER:

- Product knowledge is the foundation of sales proficiency.
- Product belief fosters conviction, enhancing sales performance.
- Product knowledge alone isn’t enough to create sales.
- Selling skills and attitude are also required.
- Selling skills affect and improve attitude.
- Attitude determines success or failure.
- The three areas of selling competency are codependent—*To be successful, you must master all of them.*

CHAPTER THREE

Selling Your Clients the Way They *Want* to Be Sold

"Clients want to sold in a manner they feel comfortable with."

Empathy versus the Drive to Succeed

The effective Partner Selling professional must possess two important qualities that, ironically, are often in contradiction with each other.

Think of it as a scale of justice. The following descriptions will tell you which side of the scale you naturally fall into.

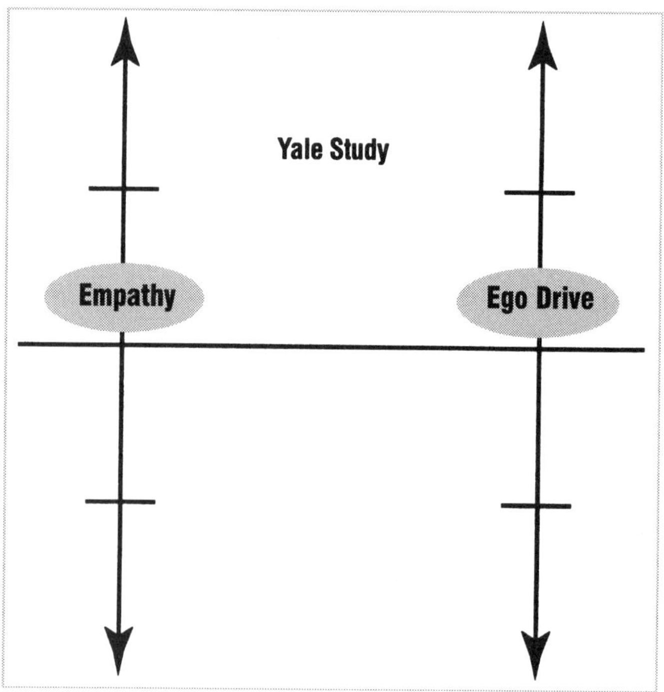

On one side of the sale is the first quality: empathy.

This can be defined as the ability to put yourself in other people's shoes, to understand where they're coming from.

It is the ability to meet total strangers and immediately establish a rapport and build a sense of trust with them.

Empathy does not necessarily extend to sympathy, nor should it.

Sympathy can be defined as both understanding a person and sharing that person's feelings.

Physicians need to empathize with their patients. But if they sympathize—say, actually share in the emotional pain of a patient to whom they've just given bad news—they lose objectivity and may cease to be effective in their role.

Empathy enables us to feel comfortable with other people and start a relationship which leads to a desire to understand their problems and concerns—the beginning of the Partner Selling process.

On the other side of the scale is the drive to succeed.

A Partner Selling professional must have this desire to achieve results.

This is the drive to get a client to make a commitment and take the appropriate next step in the sales process.

It's what enables a person to work on his or her own, to self-motivate—an essential quality for Partner Selling.

Psychologists tell us that people with a strong will to succeed require a sense of accomplishment; they need to see results fairly often in order to feel fulfilled. If you show me a group of sales people, I can virtually guarantee that the highest producers among the group are the ones with the strongest accomplishment and results orientation.

People tend naturally to be more one way than the other. They are either very empathetic and not very results-oriented, or very results-oriented and not very empathetic.

People who are very empathetic make excellent health care providers because their job is to nurture and provide support, not necessarily to produce a result.

By contrast, people with low empathy and a strong drive to achieve generally become high-pressure sales people.

Thrust a highly empathetic person into an environment where he or she must achieve difficult sales results and that person will be uncomfortable and do poorly.

Similarly, thrust a person with a strong drive to produce results into a job that has little or no accountability and that person is likely to become very frustrated, bored, and also do poorly.

This is why not everybody is capable of being a Partner Selling professional.

The most effective Partner Selling professionals must possess a balance of these two opposing characteristics.

They require, in equal measure, the empathy to "read the client," to grasp what the client needs at what time, and the drive to produce a positive result—for the client's bottom line and their own.

The Four Client Personalities and How to Respond to Them

I was in the market for a new home several years ago and went to an open house for some condominiums being built in the neighborhood I was considering.

I was chomping at the bit to get a look at the place to see whether it suited my needs. But before showing me around, the sales person working the open house insisted on running through the fine print of the real estate contract.

While the contract and its intricate details were of paramount importance to her, they were, at this stage, of little or no importance to me.

(She was a detail person and assumed I was too.)

Her selling approach was to sell me the way *she* wanted to be sold according to her personality, not the way I wanted to be sold according to mine.

I left quickly, never to return.

The moral of this story is that clients are not all alike. They make decisions differently.

In traditional selling, each person is approached the same way and goes through the same process.

Partner Selling attunes you to the individual—the first step in understanding the client, which is the cornerstone to success into today's competitive marketplace.

Sales people should never presume that just because they like to be approached a certain way, that each of their clients want to be sold in the identical manner.

Clients have different personalities. They make buying decisions differently.

They want to be heard. They want to be communicated with and ultimately sold in a manner *they* feel comfortable with.

They want sales people to get in step *with them*. To listen. And to respond to what they've heard.

Partner Selling involves mastering the art of recognizing these personality differences—and making whatever adjustments in selling technique may be necessary to respond to those differences in order to achieve the desired result: a mutually beneficial relationship.

In any selling situation, one of four distinct personalities will typically be encountered. The personalities are:

- Expressives
- Steadies
- Dominators
- Analyzers

By understanding the type of person you are selling to, it is possible to predict with some degree of accuracy how that person will respond to a specific selling approach. You, the seller, fall into one of these categories as well.

The key to recognizing which client personality you are dealing with (in order to modify your selling style accordingly and influence that client) requires some understanding of your own traits.

Stuart Serota, a lead sales person at Leviton Manufacturing Company in Little Neck, New York, and a user of the Partner Selling model, shows how modifying your selling style can lead to sales success.

"One of our largest accounts has three equal partners, a difficult situation to balance because I have to deal with three different personality types," Stuart says. "I was having particular difficulties with one of the partners because he is a Dominator, as am I. At the worst stages of our relationship, we just conducted screaming contests, which caused a great deal of friction at the account. But as a result of learning from the Partner Selling Model how to adapt my style to his by becoming more of a Steady, an active listener who lets him do most of the talking, communication between us has really improved. I'm able to steer our conversations in the direction I want to go, which has led to a better understanding of his needs and concerns. We've developed a newfound respect and courtesy for each other we'd never had before, and there are no more screaming contests. In fact, our business together has grown by 30 percent. How about that!"

Let's look at a description of each category—and the most suitable selling approach.

Expressives

There's a telling line in the movie *Beaches* when Bette Midler's character turns to Barbara Hershey's character and says, "I've talked enough about me, now what do you think of me?" That's the Expressive personality in a nutshell. It is the person who sees him or herself as the center of the universe.

Expressives view the world around them in a positive light. They are generally upbeat, enthusiastic, high-energy people.

They are very comfortable in social situations and look for opportunities to interact with others. (For example, they make very poor librarians.)

They like to be entertained and make decisions in groups.

Expressives want to be your friend and for you to like them.

They are very attentive to how they are perceived. They go for status symbols and seek out situations where they can shine in the spotlight. They are recognition-oriented.

How to Sell Expressives:

- Show interest in them as people.
- Be entertaining and fun.
- Don't hurry the decision.
- Let *them* talk.
- Direct them toward *mutually agreed upon objectives*.
- Provide testimonials.

Steadies

Somebody once said that Expressives are paid for what they *say* they do, whereas Steadies are paid for what they *actually* do.

This is a fair description of the major distinction between the two personality types, which are otherwise alike in many ways.

Steadies are upbeat, fun-loving people who view the world positively as well. But, unlike Expressives, they are more comfortable behind the scenes than in the spotlight.

Steadies are consummate empathizers.

They are very interested in and good at building and nurturing relationships.

They are caring.

They are attentive listeners.

They know how to make people relax quickly in their company.

Steadies are the workers of the world.

Statistics reveal that 42 percent of the population falls into this category. Without Steadies, the world would crumble.

Steadies are not risk-takers.

They are slow, sometimes even resistant to change.

They prefer the way things are, the status quo.

Steadies are measured and tentative in their approach to being sold. They go slowly and seek out much information before making a move.

How to Sell Steadies:

- Be pleasant and nonthreatening.
- Develop trust and credibility.
- Go slow.
- Focus them on the "human element."
- Actively listen.
- Be warm and sincere.

Dominators

Dominators view the world with suspicion. Their motto is, "I'm going to get you before you get me!"

They are almost wholly achievement-driven and seek positions of authority and power.

Statistics show that 89 percent of those in high-level management positions are Dominators.

They are demanding, impatient, and restless. They are very consumed with the bottom line and getting results. As a result, Dominators are not known for their warmth and friendliness.

I saw a sign at a company I visited once that was obviously written by a Dominator. It read: "The firings will continue until morale increases."

Dominators do not like wasting time; they're eager to get on with things. They make decisions very quickly and change their minds very slowly.

Dominators size people up rapidly. You are with them or against them. You either get in step with them right away or are thrown out into the cold.

Dominators gravitate to people who are as results-oriented as they are.

How to Sell Dominators:

- Be prepared and organized.
- Get to the point. (Be direct.)
- Demonstrate efficiency and competence.
- Uncover goals and motivations.
- Respond to *their* ideas.
- Get your facts straight.

- Provide references.
- Make your presentation quickly and the process of buying as easy for them as possible.

Analyzers

The comedienne Paula Poundstone does a routine about her father that accurately describes the Analyzer personality.

"If you ever met my father and wanted to torture him," she says, "all you would have to do is tie his hands behind his back and stand in front of him refolding a road map incorrectly. It would drive him absolutely batty."

Analyzers are the most competent of the four personality types, but the slowest to complete a task.

Analyzers view the world with suspicion. They differ from Dominators in that they are detail-oriented. In fact, they are obsessed with detail. The street phrase, of course, is "anal-retentive."

They require deadlines in order to produce.

They are fearful of criticism and do everything possible to avoid it.

They wallow in information and overdocument everything so that when they do make a decision they can justify and substantiate that decision step-by-step.

Analyzers are perfectionists by nature and love facts and details.

They do not show a lot of emotion and don't like it if you do.

They are not swayed by force of personality; on the contrary, they usually mistrust any show of enthusiasm. They feel you are trying to put one over on them.

A recent study revealed that 92 percent of all surgeons are Analyzers. (Good thing. How would you like a Dominator to operate on you?)

Analyzers make good engineers.

My accountant is an Analyzer. (Another good thing. If I were his accountant, we'd both be in jail.)

Analyzers are also very resistant to being described as Analyzers.

For example, I was speaking to the sales people of a large pharmaceutical company, many of whom were chemists in addition to being sales people. Some took umbrage at my portrait of their personality type, seeing it as very negative (which it isn't if you've been reading carefully).

As I was leaving, one of them came up to me to protest.

"I am *not* an Analyzer!" The man insisted.

I said, "Fine. It's okay."

At that, he smiled victoriously, and then proceeded to tell me there were several typos in the handouts I provided to the group—proving me right after all!

How to Sell Analyzers:

- Expect to provide a great deal of information.
- Be well-prepared and thorough.
- Ask logical, clear questions.
- Provide solid, tangible evidence of your claims.
- Give them time to think.
- Avoid pushing them.
- Follow through and exceed expectations.

To draw yourself a clear picture of the four personality types—the *Expressive*, the *Steady*, the *Dominator*, and the *Analyzer*—imagine them being trapped in a foxhole together when someone tosses in a live hand grenade. What would each do?

The *Expressive* would be out the back of the foxhole and gone before the grenade touched ground.

The *Steady* would throw himself on the grenade to save everybody.

The *Dominator* would pick up the grenade and throw it back at the enemy with a curse.

And the *Analyzer* would calculate the size of the hole the grenade would probably make when it exploded!

Most people are not all one way or the other, of course. They are usually a combination of two personality types, with one personality dominating.

The most common combinations are:

- Dominator/Expressives
- Expressive/Steadies
- Steady/Analyzers

Less common combinations are Dominator/Analyzers and Expressive/Analyzers.

Virtually unheard of is the Dominator/Steady combination, the reason for which is self-evident. Such a person would be extremely confused, almost schizophrenic, not knowing whether to mug you or hug you!

By categorizing your clients' personality types, you can determine the best way to present your product or service to them and sell them the way they want to be sold.

POINTS TO REMEMBER:

- Understanding the client is the cornerstone to building a competitive edge.
- Empathy is required to understand client problems and concerns.
- The drive to succeed is required to move the sales process forward.
- Clients want to be sold in a manner they feel comfortable with.
- Clients fall into four personality types.
- Recognizing each client's personality type and adjusting your selling approach to it is essential to your sales success.

CHAPTER FOUR

The Partner Selling Model

"Companies that recognize traditional selling techniques no longer work are the ones that will succeed."

As markets have become more complex and sophisticated, with competition up and client loyalty down, the "shoot from the hip" selling styles of the past, of relying on charm and force of personality to see you through, are no longer viable or practical. Developing a strategic approach to selling has assumed greater importance.

As a result, professional selling has changed drastically over the years, and three main methods have emerged:

Canned Selling

Often used in telemarketing situations, this approach is founded on a philosophy of attrition, which states that if you make a huge volume of sales calls, you will make sales to some of the people contacted even if the sales person's skill level is low.

Canned, or scripted, selling has become more popular because the cost of making face-to-face sales calls over the years has skyrocketed.

According to a recent study conducted by the trade publication *Sales and Marketing* magazine, the average cost of a face-to-face sales call these days is around $245. The canned selling method is a systematic method of bringing the cost of the sale down.

Using this method, a sales company can contact many more potential prospects a day in the same amount of time—and at much lower cost—than it would take for face-to-face sales calls. Canned selling requires a low level of skill and training. Therefore, the cost is lowered even more.

The problem with canned selling is that clients perceive it as both intrusive and impersonal. Unable to deviate from the generalized script, the sales person cannot personalize the pitch and does not ask individualized questions or deal with unusual responses well.

This often results in annoying interchanges that might seem amusing if the call wasn't taking place at an inopportune time—usually just as you and your family are sitting down to dinner.

I get at least one call a week from someone selling replacement windows. Each time I respond that I'm not in the market for replacement windows because my house is only four years old, the sales person just rattles on anyway with a "Yes, but . . ."

There is no but!

The sales person is so busy focusing on the script, so *married* to it, that I, the prospect, am not being heard.

This is the major downside of canned selling, which is predicated upon one all-abiding consideration—keeping costs down.

Canned selling does work in some cases and can be very helpful when combined with other forms of marketing such as direct mail, but it is not a practical method for most selling situations today simply because *clients don't respond well to it.*

Traditional Selling

I've already touched upon this selling process, but it is important to look at it again because so many companies are still using it.

It emphasizes product knowledge and can also be called a "product dump" or "features dump."

The sales person is trained to dominate the interaction between buyer and seller. Most clients are overwhelmed by it—and many sales people are too—because it creates an uncomfortable, stressful situation.

Still, traditional selling's manipulative, hard-sell tactics continue to be used more than fifty years after the process's inception.

I recently went into a large retail electronics chain to look at laptop computers. The sales person I encountered typifies the traditional selling approach and mindset.

This sales person was an Analyzer—whereas I'm an Expressive/Dominator (not the easiest mix to sell to.) For a buyer-seller interaction to be successful, the sales person must make some adjustments in selling style.

I was full of questions that never got answered because the sales person was full of product facts and figures he just couldn't wait to get out of his mouth.

What *I* wanted to know was viewed by him as less important, less urgent and critical, than what *he* wanted to tell me! I was therefore forced into the unsatisfying and uncomfortable situation of being required to adapt to *his* style—a situation that left me feeling confused, pressured, and ultimately resistant, rather than eager to buy. I felt like I'd been having an argument with him.

This approach no longer works in today's world, where clients want to be treated—and sold—as individuals.

Companies that recognize traditional selling no longer works are the ones that will succeed in the twenty-first century.

Partner Selling

This approach raises the buyer-seller interaction to the top in terms of importance.

It is built on relationships and, as a result, will always take longer to complete than canned or traditional selling methods. But the rewards, personal and financial, will be greater.

Partner Selling focuses on client needs rather than just selling products and services.

It is based on establishing an honest, trusting relationship with the buyer.

It encourages the sales person to first find out if there is a fit between the problem(s) the client seeks to resolve and the solutions(s) that the product or service they're selling can provide.

It trains the sales person to *"listen the client"* into a sale; then customize the product presentation in accordance with what is heard to make the sale and enter into a relationship.

Joe Huffman, Vice President of Distribution Sales for Leviton Manufacturing, Inc. and an important client of the Partner Selling Group, provides excellent testimony to how this works:

"We had been asked to make a capabilities presentation to a customer in the Pacific Northwest," Joe explains. "With the Partner Selling process fresh in their minds, our sales reps determined that the principal person they'd be talking to was an Analyzer-type. Realizing they had far too many capabilities and plans on their laundry list to present in the one hour allotted to them, they decided to take a more analytical approach themselves, and do more listening than talking. This sounds like such an obvious strategy when you think about it, but we are usually so intent on telling *our side* of things, especially when faced with time constraints, that we often forget to ask the customer the simple question 'How can we be of benefit to you and your company's success?'

"They were so effective that their allotted one hour turned into three. Of the eleven presentations the customer had requested from potential suppliers that week, ours, we were told, was the best. Why? Because, the customer said, we were the only supplier to even *ask* what his needs, plans, and objectives were!"

Joe concludes: "Once those items were determined, it was easy for our reps to fit the pieces of this client's particular puzzle together, review our resources, and present the right match of capabilities."

Partner Selling feels different to clients and sales people alike.

It fosters an environment where clients feel they are being treated in the way they want to be treated. It is more consistent with the way clients prefer to be sold and therefore more conducive to a mutually profitable relationship.

It is also more in tune with both the client and the sales person's personal value system.

One of my seminar students summed up the difference between traditional selling and Partner Selling very well.

She told me she always felt she wasn't manipulative or tricky enough to be successful in selling—but now realizes she doesn't have to be in order to get great results.

Ironically, most companies and their sales people believe they already practice Partner Selling.

In seminars, two of my first questions are: "Does the Partner Selling approach fit with your industry?" And "Have you adopted it?" Most respond "yes" to both questions.

PARTNER

One reason for this is that the Partner Selling technique is simple, easy to understand—and easy to remember. You can use the word PARTNER to help you recall the six steps:

P = *P*re- and Post-Planning & Prospecting
A = *A*pproaching
R = *R*eviewing Needs
T = *T*ranslating Value
N = *N*egotiating
ER = *E*ntering into *R*elationship

Let's take a quick look at each of these steps.

Pre- and Post-Planning & Prospecting—studying up on the client.

- Ascertain what you need to know about the company to get a feel for its problems and concerns and see if there is a potential match-up with your solutions.
- Gather as much information as possible about the company *and* the client/prospect you will be selling to before the face-to-face meeting, so you are fully prepared.
- Talk to company consultants, employees, your prospect's secretary, and other pertinent sources to get the information you require.
- Read the company's annual report.
- Write out some questions for the prospect before you go face-to-face, and use them to develop the outline for your prospecting script.
- Set a specific goal for your next meeting.

Approaching—meeting the client and establishing trust and rapport.

- Dress well and/or appropriately for the occasion.
- Know the person's name and how he or she prefers to be addressed.
- Memorize the names of all others involved in the meeting.
- Shake hands firmly.
- Make strong eye contact.
- Stop thinking about yourself and focus your entire attention on the client.
- Make the prospect feel relaxed and comfortable in your presence.
- Get the prospect to open up to you.
- Keep your energy level up.

Reviewing needs—identifying the opportunity for a matchup.

- Listen intently to the person you are selling.
- Ask need-development questions.
- Explore the client's past buying experiences.
- Fully understand the client/prospect's problems and concerns.
- Take notes.

Translating value—presenting needs-specific solutions.

- Make recommendations targeting the client's individual problems and concerns.
- Define how your product or service can help the client achieve his or her goals.

- Describe the long-range *value* of the product or service you offer— not just its immediate benefit.
- Communicate a strong sense of investment in the client's continued success.

Negotiating—reaching a mutual agreement.

- Deal forthrightly with the client.
- Be honest about what you *can't* do for the client, as well as what you can do.
- Probe for obstacles that may block the sale rather than wait for the client to bring them up.
- Address uncovered obstacles to the sale head-on.
- Work with the client to overcome these obstacles.

Enter into relationship—moving to the next step of confirming the beginning of a relationship.

- View the sale as an opening, not a closing.
- See yourself as a partner, not a victor.
- Set the next meeting or next action step in your current meeting.
- Recognize buying signals and ask trial close questions.

Following is a test I use to help participants in my seminars identify their existing Partner Selling skills:

Assess Your Partner Selling Skills

Read each statement and assign a rating to the box that best describes your selling habits. 1 = never; 2 = seldom; 3 = sometimes; 4 = always.

( ) I take the time to establish trust and rapport before I start translating the value of my products and services.

( ) I spend time up-front thinking about what my client's needs might be.

( ) I feel relaxed and in control of my emotions and the direction of the sale when I'm face-to-face.

( ) I spend time with the *right* prospects, those who represent both high potential and high probability of buying from me soon.

( ) I am able to get my prospects talking about themselves so I can identify their needs quickly.

( ) I am able to ask need-development questions and get the prospect to do 80 percent of the talking.

( ) I anticipate serious sales objections and ask questions about them early in my presentation.

( ) I am able to ask about sensitive financial information.

( ) I ask payoff questions as part of my needs-assessment.

( ) I prospect well and keep my pipeline full.

( ) I understand the features of my products so well that it's easy for me to translate their value to my prospects.

( ) I am able to position my products and services as clearly different from those of my competitors.

( ) I understand my competitors' strengths and weaknesses.

( ) I check my clients' reactions by observing their behavior and nonverbal signals throughout the presentation.

( ) I am able to prospect for clients without fear of rejection.
( ) I am able to identify all buying influences and adapt to them.
( ) I am an effective networker.
( ) While I'm selling, I think about my client's needs and objectives, not my need for money or reaching my quota.
( ) I am able to increase the opportunity during the sale by asking more detailed and complete questions.
( ) I can offer proof and give several reasons why my products and services are better than the competition's.
( ) I have clear goals and continually update and remind myself about them.
( ) I stop selling if I cannot find a match between my products and services and the prospect's needs.
( ) I respond to buying signals during the presentation.
( ) I ask trial closing questions to determine where the prospect is in the buying process.
( ) I have a positive view of objections and welcome them.

( ) TOTAL

Now add up your score.

80–100 points:	Your Partner Selling skills are high.
60–80 points:	You are well on your way to being a Partner Selling professional.
30–60 points:	You're making progress but have a ways to go.
1–30 points:	Turn the page and *keep reading this book*!

John D. Hall and my brother Dennis Frare are co-owners of Training Wheels, Inc., a two-year-old company in Orlando, Florida specializing in leadership training programs. John walks us through each step of the Partner Selling process and how it worked for him in the following account of a real-life situation he encountered.

"I was fortunate in that this particular client was fishing for a customer service leadership training program when he found us. A major hospital in Amarillo, Texas was undergoing rapid and complex change as a result of a merger between it and two neighboring hospitals. The president of the hospital had the foresight to recognize that the merger was not translating well into daily staff behaviors at his hospital, and he was looking for a solution.

"During a series of phone conversations with him, I was very attentive to his personality style, which I assessed as Dominator-Expressive, so I adapted my own Expressive-Steady style to accommodate him. Being direct and result-oriented with him contributed quickly to our developing a rapport that, in turn, led to our building a sense of trust.

"Prior to our first content meeting, I had rehearsed my open-ended need-development questions. This advanced preparation allowed me to focus on getting him to open up by letting him do most of the talking.

"By doing most of the listening, I was able to get a clear picture of his needs. This picture enabled me to translate the features and benefits of our customer service training program smoothly, and highlight how we might customize our program to address his needs in specific ways.

"As a by-product of pre-planning, I was able to anticipate potential objections and focus on the value-added impact of our customized program. Trial closing questions smoothly moved into a comfortable close in which we reached agreement easily and quickly.

"As a result of cultivating a 'partnership mentality,' we have fostered an ongoing mutual win-win relationship. In follow-up meetings, we have identified a menu of additional long-term needs he had in other leadership areas and customized training programs to meet them.

"Kudos to Partner Selling for providing Training Wheels with an 'un-common sense' approach to a potentially intimidating process such as selling our training programs. It is a user-friendly system that has served and will continue to serve us well."

POINTS TO REMEMBER:

- A strategic approach to selling is critical as markets become more complex and sophisticated.
- Canned selling is cost-effective, but can turn most customers off.
- Traditional selling emphasizes hard-sell tactics rather than buyer-seller partnering.
- Partner Selling focuses on client needs and long-term relationships rather than just selling products or services.
- Pre-plan your presentation by studying up on the client.
- Establish trust and rapport to get the client to open up.
- Review their needs to identify your opportunities.
- Present need-specific solutions and translate value.
- Deal with objections openly and honestly.
- Set your sights on building a relationship, not just transitory goals.

CHAPTER FIVE

Pre- and Post-Planning Your Partner Selling Presentation

"The more you know about the client beforehand, the better your odds of achieving a long-term, mutually profitable relationship."

Studying the Client

The Boy Scouts of America have a motto: "Be prepared."

It applies to Partner Selling as well.

The more information you have ahead of time about the company you will be visiting, the more you know beforehand about the decisionmaker(s) to whom you will be presenting face-to-face, the better your odds will be of successfully moving through each step of the Partner Selling process and achieving your goal. You want to achieve a matchup between your products and services and the client-company's needs, which will result in a mutually profitable and productive long-term relationship.

Knowledge Is Power

Pre-planning involves getting yourself ready to ask the right questions by asking yourself many questions up front.

It is a discipline whereby you collect as much relevant information as possible beforehand to facilitate handling almost any eventuality as you make your face-to-face presentation.

Pre-planning is the *antithesis* of the "shoot from the hip" style so common in traditional selling—and a critical first step in the Partner Selling process. In fact, it is the blueprint for your Partner Selling presentation.

Solid pre-planning not only shows the client-company how prepared and professional you are ("This person really did his or her homework!"), it makes the client-prospect *feel* that you really care about doing business with him or her.

The nature and complexity of the product or service you provide determines the quantity and types of information you should strive to gather ahead of time.

A good rule of thumb, however, is that "more is *always* better than less."

My friend Geoffrey Riddle, an experienced sales person who had previously sold insurance and financial services for eighteen years, switched careers and purchased a Cousins Sub franchise in Phoenix, Arizona. In talking with other franchisees in the food service business, it quickly became apparent to Geoff that most of them competed toe-to-toe for customers by offering coupons and large discounts on big catering orders. From past experience, nothing was more distasteful to Geoff than having to "bid" on business, a situation that results in price alone becoming the determining factor in who gets the sale. His competitors were perfectly willing to sacrifice profits for potential future sales and market recognition, even though this strategy didn't appear to be working for them. To cut costs, many of them had started using inferior, low-cost ingredients in their food.

"I was very confident in the quality of our subs, but knew I couldn't compete for the big catering orders on price alone," Geoff says. So, he tried a different tactic. "Because of my background in insurance, I knew that most insurance companies held sales meetings in which food was served," Geoff says. "So, I did a little research. I called one of them to gather vital information about regular meetings like the purpose of the meetings, the results expected from them, if food was served, who bought it, from where, how much they paid, and so on.

"It turned out that this company used food as a major incentive to get staff members to attend sales meetings. One of my competitors was already supplying the sub sandwiches for these meetings, having gotten the account because they were cheaper than anyone else around. Because they were using inferior ingredients in their subs in order to cut costs and be cheaper, their subs unfortunately weren't proving to be much of a come-on since weekly attendance at these sales meetings remained weak. I saw an opportunity and decided to seize it.

"When calling on potential customers, it's recommended by the franchiser that we wear a logo-ed shirt and baseball cap for brand identification," Geoff says. "But such casual dress is a no-no with certain industries which remain very much shirt and tie, and I knew from experience that insurance was one of them, so I wore a sport jacket and tie to my first face-to-face. I couldn't compete on price, so I didn't try to meet or beat that of my competitor. Instead, armed with the knowledge that the customer used food to boost attendance at sales meetings, and that this strategy wasn't working with the current supplier, I made the company's sale manager an offer: serve *our* subs at this week's meeting, and if attendance didn't spike up the following week, there would be no charge."

It worked, Geoff says. "After the first meeting where our subs were served, it became evident that word had gotten around the office that the quality of the food had improved because our order for the following week was more than double what we had originally provided. Weekly attendance at these meetings picked up and I got a new customer without having to discount my product, a win-win for both of us. And it all grew out of doing my homework, of following through with some solid pre-planning."

Here's more evidence. Mike Arnoff is President of Arnoff Moving and Storage, a well-established logistics company in New York State and longtime client of the Partner Selling group. "We recently called on an account in the New England area for which we had previously performed two North American relocations that year that had gone quite well, only to find out this company had no more such relocations planned," Mike says. "However, we were aware in advance through our research that this company was also in the international market, so we were loaded for bear and the meeting did not end there. We jumped right into our international proposal and presented it in a manner that provided the client with the assurance that we were a total relocation company capable of anticipating and handling all its overseas market needs as well. We've had a contract for this client's North American *and* international relocation business ever since."

Mike concludes that, "If we had not been prepared, had not done our research, we would have been deflated immediately and unable to press on."

Locating Information

Finding what you need to know ahead of time about a client or company to sufficiently prepare yourself can be achieved in a number of ways.

One of the easiest is to place a phone call to the prospect and have a friendly, introductory chat with his or her secretary.

You can get a general line on what the boss is like, personally and professionally (Expressive, Steady, Dominator, Analyzer) so you can make the appropriate adjustment to your selling style.

Ask for the names and phone numbers of any other very important top officers (VITO) with whom you will be dealing when you get there—and what they are like personally and professionally. In fact, you might want to pick up a copy of

Tony Parinello's *Selling to VITO*, which describes the art of prospecting for this type of information in great detail.

Request the secretary to send you a copy of the company's latest annual report. This will tell you a considerable amount about the company's history, profit picture, goals, objectives, and people.

If it is a publicly traded company, you might get some of this data, as well as a copy of the annual report, right in your local public library—a reliable though often neglected source of information about companies and businesses.

Up-front knowledge of the client-company's competitive picture is another essential ingredient to effective pre-planning.

Who are the company's competitors?

Does the client-company already have a competitive edge in the marketplace that your product or service might strengthen or expand?

Is the client-company currently suffering a competitive disadvantage that your product or service might remove?

What general client needs can you ascertain beforehand?

This up-front knowledge will get you focused on asking need-development questions when you get face-to-face—and asking the right ones.

By knowing what some of these questions are, and preframing some of them beforehand, you increase the likelihood of remembering to bring all of them up.

What objections might you anticipate that could prevent the process from moving forward to the next step?

Anticipating possible objections is key to adequate preparation for dealing with them if or when they come up.

Prospecting

In the movie *Annie Hall,* Woody Allen's character describes relationships as being like a shark. If they don't keep moving, they die. So it is with clients and customers. If you fail to keep moving on to new prospects, you won't add many new clients and customers to your base and increase sales, you'll just be dealing with the ones you have, you'll come to a standstill, and you'll ultimately wind up with a dead shark on your hands.

Prospecting for new business is thus one of the most important elements of the sales process and a valuable skill sales people must possess. Sales people need to be able to prospect well in order to avoid growing stale, to feel productive in their work, and most important to keep generating new business opportunities. If they are unable to expand their prospects, after a while they'll run out of clients and customers, which is not exactly the road to riches.

For example, one of my clients, Leviton Manufacturing Company, makes innovative and quality wiring devices for commercial buildings and residential homes. Traditionally, the company has sold its products through a network of distributors who serve the end user, in this case the building trade. Since these distributors also handle the products of Leviton's competitors, the company recognized that in order to gain a competitive edge and grow the business, it had to expand its prospects. Thus, the company has decided to have its sales people start calling directly on the end users, the architects themselves, in an effort to get them to go to the distributor and specify Leviton's wiring devices for the buildings they're designing.

Getting an appointment to sit down, tell your story, and find out if there's a match with a prospective client or customer you've never sold to before is something you as a sales person must do, and do well. It not only requires confidence and skill, but a methodology, a formula that can be followed that will ensure at least a reasonable chance of success.

I've come up with such a formula. It is designed to help companies like Leviton enhance their prospecting skills and improve their success rate in those all-important telephone calls to set up appointments with potentially valuable new prospects. A microcosm of my Partner Selling Model, it consists of three pre-planning steps that should be adhered to in sequence in order to bring about the best results.

The Partner Selling Prospecting System

STEP 1: PRIORITIZE YOUR PROSPECTS.

To be a successful sales person, you have to be astute in identifying the *best opportunities* for new business. Identifying the best opportunities involves carefully researching and prioritizing your list of prospects so that you spend the bulk of that precious commodity called time on maximum advantage. In other words, "Don't major in the minors," or, put yet another way, don't spend major amounts of time on prospects who will likely yield only minor gains.

The way to do this is to lay as much groundwork as possible before reaching for the phone, starting with evaluating your pipeline and placing a value grade, based on a specific set of criteria, on each prospect category you've identified as being a potentially good candidate for new business.

Knowledge of your existing customers will help you know what to look for in identifying prospects and in establishing this criteria, so you'll have a firm idea which direction you should be going in.

The value grades you set can be as simple as the letters A, B, and C, with each letter representing a description, or profile, of the prospect and a determination of which category it falls into based on the criteria you've established.

Criteria you should use in making that A, B, or C determination might be the prospect client or company's:

- Size
- Need
- History of purchasing products like yours
- Volume or quantity of such purchases
- Geographic location
- SIC code

Ask yourself ahead of time:

"Who are my prospective clients and customers?"
"What do they look like?"
"How will I recognize them when I see them?"
"Will it really be worth my while to pursue this prospect?"
"Is there a strong possibility the prospect is someone I'll want to do business with if I invest that time?"

All of these questions must be asked and answered up front, your criteria predetermined and continually re-evaluated, *before* you ever pick up the phone. The reason why is simply this: You want to be sure you're not spending more time on prospects who present only minimal opportunity.

Think of your pipeline as a funnel. You pour each prospect into the top, or widest part, of the funnel, but only a few will emerge at the bottom as qualified new business opportunities. You have to review each prospect's needs and assess the potential for a win-win outcome. This is how you move each prospect down through your funnel, evaluating it as an A, B, or C priority.

Remember, in order to keep your pipeline full, it's important to continually add more prospects to that funnel. Only in this way can you hope to have more of them come out at the bottom as bona fide new clients and customers.

Step 2: Predetermine Two Ideal Times for Your Appointment.

Now that you have a clear picture of who your prospects are and have established the order in which you want to call on them—the "A" candidates being potentially the "hottest," the "C" list being more "iffy"—so as to make the best use of your time, you may feel you're ready to start dialing. Not just yet! There are a few more pre-planning steps to go through if you want to increase your batting average at getting appointments with prospects on the phone.

The second step is to look at your calendar and preselect the two most convenient times for your appointment with the prospect. For example, if you're going to be in the prospect's vicinity on other business over a Tuesday and Wednesday of the following week, plan to suggest meeting with him or her during your free time either of those two days. Be very selfish here. Predetermine when it is in *your best interest* to meet with the prospect, not the other way around, and fix those dates in your mind before you call.

The reason for scheduling this way is that to be a successful sales person, you must be very good at managing your time effectively. It's absolutely critical for you to keep as much control over your schedule as possible and not have others controlling it for you.

On eight out of ten occasions—a very high percentage of the time—the prospect will easily agree to meet with you during one of your two predetermined appointment dates.

You must be flexible, of course. If the prospect simply can't meet with you either of those times, you'll have to quickly make other arrangements—in which case, suggest two alternate dates when you know you'll be in his or her location.

The key here is to run your professional life according to *your* time management system, not someone else's, or the prospect's. (For more on time and territory management, see Chapter 11.)

STEP 3: PREPARE YOUR SCRIPT OUTLINE.

Now you have to preplan not only *what* you want to say when you get the prospect on the phone, but equally important, *how* you want to say it.

Prospects are busy people, just like you, and may get a lot of calls like yours, including pesky ones from business-to-business telemarketers trying to sell them something. You won't have a lot of time to grab their attention, probe them for information, and present your case. So, get to it quickly.

Succinctly Introduce Yourself and Your Company.

Since the prospect really doesn't care who you are at this point and undoubtedly has many other things on his or her mind, identify yourself quickly, clearly, concisely in a business-like but friendly manner, then swiftly move on. For example: "Mr. Prospect, I'm Bob Frare from the Partner Selling Group."

Briefly State the Reason for Your Call and Then Ask Permission to Proceed.

Be clear and concise about why you're calling—and why it's in the prospect's interest to keep listening—by making a quick, *general* statement about the value your company has added to companies similar to the prospect's with whom you've done business. Then, and this is very important, conclude this statement by seeking the prospect's permission to continue the conversation. The biggest mistake made by sales people cold calling prospects on the phone is to keep yakking away. I call this "steamrolling," and it is usually done out of fear that the prospect may interject something that the sales person is unprepared to answer or deal with. It usually results in the prospect simply hanging up. By following my formula, however, you will have no such fears because your pre-planning will have prepared you for every possible response in advance. Ending your reason for calling statement by asking permission to continue is not only polite, respectful, and professional, it makes the prospect feel more important than you are, and consequently inclined to make you feel equally important by granting you permission. Here's an example: "I've worked with many companies like yours and have dramatically increased their distribution effectiveness. Is now a good time to talk?" Or, "Do you have a moment to talk now?"

Conduct a Quick Needs-Assessment.

Having been given permission by the prospect to continue, which will happen most of the(time simply because you were courteous enough to ask, the next thing you want to do is conduct a quick needs-review and collect some information that will help you determine the following:

Is this prospect for you?
Is this prospect someone you want to and should meet with?
Is there a potential need here that you might be able to fulfill that will lead to a win-win opportunity?

You're on the phone, remember; you don't have a lot of time, so this must be done fast. In advance of your call, prepare three open-ended needs-review questions to ask at this stage in order to get the prospect to reveal some important things to you about his or her business situation. In other words, here is where you want the prospect to do most of the talking, and for you to do most of the listening. Always use interrogative words like "what," "when," "where," "why," and "how" as your openers. For example:

> *"How have your sales been trending lately?"*
> *"Have your sales people been meeting your level of expectations?"*
> *"Where do you see some room for improvement?"*

The answers you receive will not only help you determine if indeed this prospect is a viable one—i.e., is someone you really want to see, which is very important since you can't afford to see everybody—they will also help provide a natural segue into the next step in your script outline.

Translate Value from What You've Learned.

Earlier, when you identified yourself and the reason for your call, you provided a general statement about the value you've contributed to the bottom line of companies similar to the prospects with whom you've worked—a door opener, as it were, aimed at making the prospect want to hear more. Now it's time to get down to the brass tacks of offering some value specifics keyed to what you've learned from your brief needs-review—assuming, of course, what you've learned has indicated a possible match for a win-win opportunity. In other words, here is where you quickly raise the stakes by telling the prospect *why* he or she should grant you an appointment. In terms the prospect can understand, appreciate, and identify with, translate the value of your offering by providing some real-world details about what you've done for similar companies, how you accomplished it, and the results you achieved. For example:

> *"We put on a three-day selling strategies seminar with follow-up training for the employees of XYZ Company, and increased their productivity by 30 percent."*
>
> *"We worked with XYZ Company to put procedures in place to decrease insurance costs, which have since dropped by 20 percent."*

Since you've already done some preliminary homework on the prospect's company, have a general idea of what it does, the kind of business pressures it typically experiences, and how you may be able to help, it's a good idea to prepare several of these value-specific statements beforehand. This way you avoid having to wing it should the prospect prove to be less than revealing during the needs-review. In reality, in cold calls like these a reticent response is more common than one where a prospect is willing to tell you everything you want to know about his or her business. There are probably two or three brief but value-specific statements you can make about yourself and your offering that *may not* grow out of what the prospect tells you. But be flexible enough to be able to adapt them to what the prospect *may* tell you. And remember, neither these statements nor the entire script outline itself should simply be read to the prospect over the phone, or you will quickly hear the line go *click*! They're to serve as a guide, or coach-sheet, only.

Ask for the Appointment.

Now you're ready to do what is commonly referred to in sales lingo as "ask for the order," the order in this case being the appointment to meet with the prospect. If you become a truly adept phone prospector, it is not inconceivable that, at this stage, the prospect will actually express a wish to make an appointment to meet with you! It happens, though not frequently. This is why you predetermined those two ideal appointment times in Step 2; here is where you propose them. Another reason why I suggest that you pick *two* ideal appointment dates rather than only one is this: By giving the prospect an either/or alternative, or *ultimate choice,* it makes it much more difficult for the prospect to assume command, or say "no." Here are some examples of how to propose your ideal appointment times:

> *"I'm going to be in your vicinity early in the week. Would Tuesday or Wednesday morning be best for you?"*
>
> *"I'm free on Friday, would Friday morning be good, or would a little later in the day fit your schedule better?"*

The goal you're trying to achieve is to build as much value for your product or service as possible in a short amount of time in order to get the prospect to *want to see you.* You do this by being *proactive* rather than *reactive* every step of the way—by doing as much as you can to control the situation, from before you pick up the phone right up to the moment when you ask for thc appointment, and therefore increase your chances of success.

Call it what you will—a methodology, a formula, or a 3-Step process for effective prospecting—following it will help you accomplish your goals. Practice makes perfect. Done well, it will enable you to continually add to your pipeline, increase your win-win opportunities, and grow your bottom line.

Put It in Writing.

Before visiting a prospective client-company, I complete a form I've created that helps me see, in black and white, what I know about the prospective client-company on whom I will be calling, what my objective is, and how I intend to go about achieving that objective.

This "Partner Selling Pre-plan Form" provides me with a wealth of information on the client-company I will be approaching, a well-rounded profile that will assist me in covering as many bases as possible so that I am well prepared for my face-to-face sales call.

In effect, this "Partner Selling Pre- and Post-Planning Form" serves as my road map. It shows me where I'm going—and later on, where I've been.

I recommend filling out this form to both individual sales professionals and sales people involved in team selling situations. In addition, I've outlined some record-keeping ideas for post-planning in a later chapter—and some of the technology available that will make this task easier.

If, for example, somebody else in your company will eventually be getting involved in the sale, or you leave and someone else in your company assumes your former role with the client, your company has a written record of what has transpired. It helps communicate an all-important sense of continuity to the client, a big demand these days.

Clip it out. Make multiple copies for yourself and your associates. *Use it.*

Andrew W. Goodale, Assistant National Sales Manager of MBIA Municipal Investors Service Corporation, a leading SEC-registered investment adviser and provider of investment management programs for governments throughout the United States based in Armonk, New York, and a longtime Partner Selling Group client, sums up the value of the planning step of the Partner Selling process this way.

"Pre-planning and post-planning are critical skills for success," he says. "Since one of the best sources of marketplace information is prospects, planning what you will ask and then capturing the response is vital to accumulating knowledge. Anecdotes from a prospect are a perfect way to refine value in the minds of other prospects. What works in the 'reviewing needs' step can be captured after the call to be used again at the appropriate time in the next sales call. In this way, pre- and post-planning assures that each sales call is a resource one can build upon."

Andy then describes how he and Tom Jordan, MBIA's Director and National Sales Manager, applied this technique when launching a new government investment management program in California:

"We were visiting various prospects during a weeklong trip. One prospect, a Steady, was unsure about our program and dubious that two New Yorkers could help improve the way he invested. Happily, he was not the first prospect we visited. An earlier appointment had been with a Dominator, who spent much of the meeting sharing with us the many potential uses that she saw for our program. Using the Partner Selling pre-

Partner Selling Pre-Planning Form

Name: ______________________________

Client Company: ______________________________

Prospect(s): ______________________ Style: ____________

Address: ______________________________

Phone: ____________________ Fax: ____________________

E-Mail: ____________________

Administrative Assistant: ______________ Style: ____________

Objective of Meeting: ______________________________

____

____

Need-development questions I will ask: ______________________

____

____

Three problem areas I will focus on: ______________________

____

____

Value I can translate: ______________________________

____

____

Who are their competitors? ______________________________

____

____

Other information ______________________________

____

____

and post-planning procedures, we had captured those concrete examples of program value, which enabled us to translate value easily in our subsequent meeting with the Steady. We offered him two real-life situations faced by his office and transitioned to value with 'We've been speaking with other government officials, and they think that our program would be very helpful for . . .'

"The strategy worked. His interest level and engagement in the meeting instantly increased. On the way out, after setting our next meeting, he praised us for our thorough understanding of the needs of his marketplace. We have always prided ourselves on having in-depth market knowledge, but being able to record instances of value and then planning to use them in later appointments has helped us enormously in demonstrating the value of our programs."

POINTS TO REMEMBER:

- The more you know about a potential client ahead of time, the better your odds of success.
- Pre-planning shows potential clients you're professional and care about doing business with them.
- Talk to their secretaries to find out what clients are like. Read the annual report.
- Know both *your* competition—and your potential client's competition.
- Anticipate objections and prepare to deal with them.
- Keep your prospecting pipeline full.
- Outline your prospecting strategy.
- Create and maintain a written record.

CHAPTER SIX

Approaching Clients the Partner Selling Way

"Establish yourself as an ally in the client's eyes."

Meeting the Client and Establishing Trust and Rapport

The next step in the Partner Selling process is approaching the client face-to-face. Here is where you lay the foundation for building trust and rapport, where you establish yourself as a credible professional—your client's ally.

Achieving this goal involves many tangibles as well as intangibles.

The way we "look," "act," and "dress"—the *intangibles*—play as much a part in building trust and rapport as the "words" we use—the *tangibles*.

Even your accessories can be subtle indicators of how you feel about yourself and the client on whom you are calling. An old, battered briefcase in your hand communicates one message, a shiny new one a very different message.

Knowing When to Be On

As the saying goes: "*Knowing when to act enthusiastic is the first step to becoming enthusiastic.*"

Media expert Roger Ailes tells a great story about the late comedian Jack Benny in his book *You Are the Message.*

Early in his career, Ailes worked as a "greeter," the person who prepares guests for appearances on TV interview shows. Benny was one of them.

Benny arrived at the studio with a loose tie, his shirt collar in disarray, and seeming very lethargic, almost ill. Ailes was worried that Benny might be unable to go on. But it was too late to make a substitution. Airtime was in thirty seconds. When he told Benny this, the comedian suddenly stood erect, fixed his tie and collar, and suddenly became flushed with energy. He then proceeded to walk onto the set looking and acting fresh as a daisy.

Ailes was astonished by the transformation, by what Benny had done. In effect, the comedian had been reserving his strength, storing his energy and enthusiasm so that he could summon it at the precise moment when he needed it most to project the "Jack Benny" image.

Sales people must learn to do the same.

Many times I find myself in a situation where I am scheduled to make a sales call, but just don't feel like it.

I've got a cold and am not feeling very well. Or, it's just a beautiful day and I'd rather be playing golf instead.

What I do is take a few moments to collect myself, to focus myself on bringing my energy level up for the moment when it will be needed—so that when I go in to make the sales call, the client will have no idea how I'd really been feeling just a few minutes before.

Knowing *when* to be "on" enables you to summon what's needed at the critical time—and keeping up your energy during the interview is needed to project the desired image.

In other words, you need to create the image you want in your mind, and then *act that way*.

The Importance of Nutrition and Fitness

One tool that is often overlooked by sales people in keeping up their energy is a healthy body.

How your body performs and how you feel about your body both have a direct impact on your ability to project the image you desire in the sales arena.

The old adage "You are what you eat" has never been truer.

As most of us know, too much fat in our diets increases our chances of getting cancer, suffering a heart attack, or developing diabetes. A fat body lowers a person's energy level and reduces stamina—essential ingredients in Partner Selling.

Psychologically, if you are unhappy with the way you look and feel, you probably can't be the successful sales performer you want to be.

It is difficult to fit exercise into a busy schedule and not always easy to eat healthy when you travel a great deal, as many sales people do.

But I believe we have to find a way to accomplish this if we expect to reach our highest potential as sales people.

There are YMCAs, gyms, and parks in every city and town across the country, of which you can take advantage for a low fee.

There you can always catch an exercise class, swim a few laps, take a walk, or go for a run to improve your cardiovascular system, build muscle tone, and lower body fat composition.

Many hotels have VCRs in the rooms.

Perhaps you can bring along an exercise tape with you on the road. (*Please* consult your physician before starting any type of physical workout or training program.)

Awaken a little earlier each day, and you will have time to get in twenty or thirty minutes of workout before heading out to do business.

If you do this, you'll find you have a lot more energy and a more optimistic attitude toward the challenges you will face each day.

If you take the time to read about nutrition or meet with a dietitian or nutritionist, you can change your eating habits so that you reduce body fat, have more energy, and improve your immune system.

The result of these efforts will be a better self-image, a healthier body, and more than enough energy to successfully achieve your Partner Selling goals! (For some recommended reading on this all-important subject see Appendix V.)

Dressing for Success

Dressing appropriately is another important element in the approach formula. Clothes may make the man or woman, but they don't make the sale if they're wrong.

I always consider my schedule before getting dressed in the morning.

What type of business will I be going to?
Should I dress up, or down?
What's the personality type of the client I will be approaching?
How should I look?

I want that client to see in me the personification of the individual he or she would go to if looking for professional advice about the business.

This requires empathy as well as the knowledge acquired during the pre-planning step. I want the person to feel immediately comfortable with the image I project.

A very successful client of mine recently called on some people in the construction business. He can dress "to the nines" and owns a Cadillac. But when he calls on clients in his professional capacity at their construction sites, he always shows up in gabardines and boots driving a rusty old Chevy.

He "reads" his clients. He not only dresses for the occasion but drives for it as well in order to project the right image.

He "does his homework" in order to make the impression that he is exactly the right person with whom they can feel comfortable and confident about entrusting their business. Thus he represents himself as one of them.

(He also knows that the first minute or two of the sales call is *the* critical period for establishing this.)

Easing Sales Pressure

In my seminars, I ask, "When does a sales person begin to put pressure on the client?"

The response I get is always the same: "During the negotiation and close."

Perhaps yes. But it may also make sense to begin earlier in the process.

Sales pressure typically begins much, much sooner—sometimes during the face-to-face approach step.

In fact, some clients feel pressured just by having the sales person show up in the first place.

Alan Friedman, sales representative for Bard Interventional Products and a recent recipient of his company's President's Club Award for his new business development skills in his first year there, reveals this telling story: "I had been 'prospecting' a new client who works as Materials Coordinator at a medical center in Staten Island, New York, for some time. It took months of persistence to get him to finally return my calls, and when I met him, he didn't exactly greet me with 'open arms.'

"I first utilized the 'Approach Step' of the Partner Selling process by asking questions and not pushing my product," Alan goes on. "It was important to earn his trust before even discussing what I wanted to sell him in order to ease his feelings of sales pressure. Sales, I knew, would come in time. I then moved into the 'Review Needs' step and repeated back everything he told me, paraphrasing his words, not only to gain a clear understanding of his wants and needs but to show him I was listening, and establish myself not just as a sales person but as a true consultant on his issues. My proof that I'd succeeded in achieving all the above aims was the big smile on his face that expressed his gratitude for my patience in listening to him and not 'putting on the pressure.' Due to the correct use of these two steps alone, he and I eventually signed a contract worth more money that I had initially anticipated, and we continue to have a working partnership to this day."

At some point, the seller *must* apply a certain degree of pressure on the buyer, or the sale will go nowhere. It just will not happen.

Even though they dislike sales pressure, clients expect it. The key is to make the client view such pressure *positively,* not negatively.

This can only be achieved if the sales person has successfully built trust and rapport with the client first.

The higher the level of trust and rapport you have established with clients, the greater your credibility will be and the more they'll know you are of value to them.

Approach

When trust and rapport are high,
sales pressure is perceived to be low,
even when it is not.

TRUST, RAPPORT

↓

SALES PRESSURE

The more credibility you have, the less the client will feel the sales pressure.

Conversely, when trust, rapport, and credibility are low, clients feel uneasy and sense sales pressure when there is none. The sale is then in immediate jeopardy.

Getting clients to talk about themselves as soon as possible is an excellent way to head off this problem. It helps them relax (the first step in building rapport) and it lowers whatever unease about sales pressure they may have.

One method I use is to look for something positive to comment upon as soon as I arrive at the place of business.

For example, if a potential client's executive assistant, secretary—even receptionist—has been especially courteous and helpful to me, I'm quick to point this out to the client. I might ask, "How do you get your people to act so professionally?"

In this case my underlying message was to imply that the client was very skilled and perceptive at choosing the right people for the job. This prompted the client to start talking about how he or she performed such a critical task so successfully.

This gets the client talking about him- or herself.

In the process, I gain insight into the client's behavior style; exposing additional points of discussion I can seize on and explore later to further our relationship.

Remembering Names

The importance of remembering a prospect's name in building trust and rapport cannot be overstated. When I ask in my seminars, "how many people have difficulty remembering the names of their new clients and prospects?" 100 percent of the hands go up. Some of them even have trouble remembering the names of clients they see often and have known for a long time.

Sales people call on so many clients and prospects that remembering names is a big problem.

This is especially true in situations where sales people encounter multiple contacts with whom they must deal in a single meeting.

Remembering names is a skill sales people must master in order to help them be effective.

The first step is recognizing that it is physiologically impossible to remember a person's name if you don't hear it.

What do I mean by this?

Sales people view difficulty in remembering names as a memory problem. In reality, for most it's a *listening* problem.

Typically, sales people are so focused on their own agenda when they meet a client or prospect for the first time that they simply do not hear what is said to them initially—which is usually the person's name.

Step one: When meeting a new client, or multiple clients, you must stop thinking about yourself, about your own goals and agenda; you must unclutter your mind so you can listen.

Step two: Repeat the person's name aloud after it's spoken to you. This *forces* you to hear it.

In other words, if the prospect says, "Hello, I'm John Blake," don't respond, "Nice to meet you." Respond: "Nice to meet you, *John.*"

Getting the person's card helps.

Writing the person's name down when you are introduced is also helpful, though not always convenient, and virtually impossible when you are meeting several people simultaneously.

Step three: Quickly form a mental association as you hear each person's name.

For example, I was recently introduced to a new client whose first name is Dona. My sister's name is Donna. Same name, different spelling. Whenever I call on this client, I think of my sister, and, *boom*, the association brings the client's name right back to me.

POINTS TO REMEMBER:

- Focus totally on the person you are meeting.
- Recognize the importance of body language and other nonverbal cues in presenting the image you desire.
- Reserve energy until it's needed.
- Make an initial positive observation that gets the person talking about him or herself.
- Master the skill of remembering names.
- Build trust and rapport.

CHAPTER SEVEN

Reviewing the Client's Needs to Determine a Win-Win Outcome

"When sales people become convinced there is a match between the client's problem and their solution, it fuels them to move forward with conviction."

Identifying the Opportunity for a Matchup

A longtime friend and client of mine, Jim DeBerry, runs a successful company that sells products and services to the beauty industry.

Using the Partner Selling system, he changed his company's focus from "just selling the product" to building win-win relationships with his key clients on a partnering basis.

The partnering philosophy helped Jim's clients' businesses as well as his own business, which sells millions of dollars of products and services to them, grow and prosper.

The results of using this process have been demonstrable for Jim. And yet one day a member of his sales staff who was not having much success with clients came to him and said, "I need something to get my clients to buy. Are there any tricky questions I can ask?" As Jim said to me afterwards: *"Some people just don't get it."*

Selling shouldn't have to be based on trick questions. Once you have established trust and rapport with the prospect and gotten the person to feel relaxed and comfortable in your presence, you're ready to move to the next level—reviewing the prospect's needs by asking questions that focus on his or her needs.

In this step the prospect does most of the talking and you do a lot of listening as he or she responds to your need-development questions.

It is here where you begin to find out if there is a real opportunity for a match between the prospect's needs and what you sell.

Hal Allen has been in the financial planning industry since 1985, and is the President of Allen Financial Consultants, Inc., a full-service independent financial consulting firm located in Clifton Park, New York. He is a good friend and trusted partner.

Early in 1997, a gentleman came into his office in need of financial planning and investment management advice. "He told me he had $250,000 to invest," Hal says. "I allowed him to do most of the talking, telling me about himself, his financial situation, and exactly what he wanted and didn't want. In the course of reviewing his needs, I learned that he liked to be part of the decision-making process; in fact, he wanted to learn as much as possible about how financial decisions are made, and the reasons behind them. I assessed him as an Analyzer.

"A week later, he returned for our next meeting. I presented him with my recommendations for coordinating all of his finances and investment portfolio plus two alternative options. I explained the reasons behind each of these strategies and asked him what he thought. After answering a few of his questions, he said, 'I like it . . . it makes perfect sense. Let's do it.' Then he added: 'But there's just one thing we need to change. The amount of money I have to invest isn't $250,000 but roughly $2,000,000!' "

Hal learned afterwards that the man had been to two other financial consultants prior to going to Hal. "He became my client because I made an effort to understand his personality, and effectively reviewed his needs," Hal says. "I was able to convincingly show him how I could help by presenting my plan to him in a way he could relate to, and, as a result, the opportunity for me grew into a bigger one than I had thought. The best part is that that opportunity came about not because I *sold* him, but because he *bought* me!"

Finding the Right Pace

One way to look at the interview is as a continuum along which the prospect is steadily moved from responding to easy, low-risk types of need-development questions to answering higher-risk, payoff-oriented questions.

You can begin by asking low-risk need-development questions to get the prospect talking and used to being led by your questioning. Developed in the Partner Selling Pre-Planning stage, these questions are aimed at determining a match between needs and solutions.

As prospects begin to open up, it becomes increasingly easier to get them to reveal the details you need to know in order to discover a basis for helping solve their problems and challenges. This is the goal you should always keep in mind during your interview.

Your insight into a prospect's personality style and your ability to adjust to it assumes crucial importance in determining the pace of your questioning.

With Expressives your pace will be slower because they love to talk.

The pace with Steadies will be a bit quicker.

With results-oriented Dominators, you'll want to get to the point right away; therefore you will rapidly move to the high-risk area.

Analyzers require a different pace and a different style of needs-review altogether because they demand more detailed questions from you and provide more detailed answers.

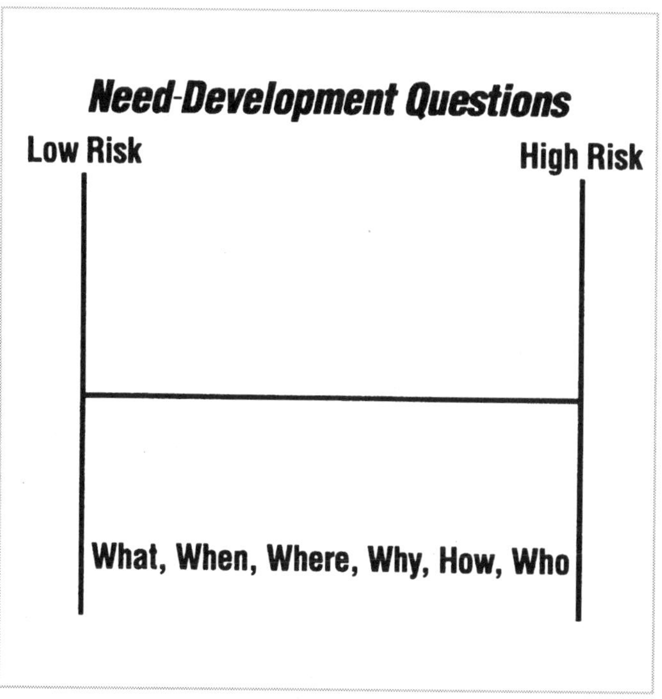

Selling Yourself First

As you move along the continuum, the need-development questions you ask are ultimately designed to uncover the existence of a legitimate match between the business problem(s) the prospect is looking to solve and the solution your product or service can provide.

When sales people become convinced there is a match, they are fueled in a way that generates energy and motivates them to move forward. For many, this is an important reason to be in sales.

This psychological response is the core of the Partner Selling system.

It merges the sales person's strong product belief with an equally strong belief that the product is the right solution to the client's problems.

It fosters the sense of *conviction* the sales person requires to proceed—that allows him or her to proceed.

In effect, reviewing the client's needs is the step whereby sales people sell themselves, where they give themselves permission to continue, and they can do so with tremendous direction, feeling both eloquent and persuasive.

The conviction that you genuinely have the solution your prospect seeks—that you can really *help* the client—is extremely important today when so many businesses are requiring so many more of their employees to assume sales functions they've never been called upon to perform before.

Nontraditional sales people are inevitably uncomfortable in such roles to begin with—and become even more so when urged to use traditional selling methods requiring them to be tricky, manipulative, and high-pressured.

Such methods don't fit right. They don't *feel* right to them.

They want and need a system that enables them to feel comfortable about what they are doing, at ease doing it, and confident that it will help them be more effective.

Partner Selling intrinsically *feels right* to nontraditional sales people. Its methods conform to their values and their belief systems. It is the way they would want to be sold and the way they want to sell.

It enables them to sell themselves first so they can then sell the prospect with total conviction.

I was asked to speak on Partner Selling to the sales staff of a company that manufactures automated office equipment for doctors and dentists. As part of my preparation, I joined the sales people beforehand for a meeting in which they were introduced to the company's new line of equipment by the vice-president of sales.

As I listened, I kept hearing the VP say things to the group like: "This new model pretty much has most of the old bugs worked out." And "What happened with the old models will never happen again."

I drew the obvious inference from this that the company had experienced significant trouble with its older line of equipment.

Before my seminar, I cornered the VP and asked him what that problem was and he said, "Oh, didn't I tell you? Our equipment has a history of going down. Last time, they screwed up billing for the 3,000 doctors and dentists who bought them from us, sending the wrong bills out to patients and so on. But we think we have that fixed. Now, please go in and motivate my sales people."

Can you imagine what those sales people were going through—having to go out into the marketplace and say to prospects that their products offered great results when, in fact, they didn't?

You cannot motivate people by making them behave in a way that is inconsistent with their values. What fuels sales people is the unshaken belief that they have something of value to sell.

Asking Revealing Questions

The goal of the needs-review is to get prospects talking specifically about the problems they want to solve—in part by doing 80 percent of the talking.

To accomplish this goal, the need-development questions the sales person asks should be somewhat open-ended—that is to say, specifically designed to elicit a response that requires explanation and elaboration that may lead to the discovery of opportunities. This can also lead to add-on sales.

Bill Anderson, Branch Manager of the Savings Institute Bank in Connecticut and a Partner Selling alumnus, had a prospect walk into his office one day to, in the prospect's words, "just gather some information."

Relates Bill: "As we spoke further, he told me that his current bank had merged with a bigger bank and closed down the branch he did business with. I assured him we would be able to provide him with what he needed, but he was somewhat reluctant to make a commitment. Instead of trying to 'push' him into opening an account with us, I kept asking questions, listening carefully to what he said, and he gradually revealed his biggest concern. His business, he indicated, was seasonal; he was concerned about not being able to maintain a certain balance in his checking account during the winter months and being assessed a higher service charge because of this. I told him that we would offer him free commercial checking for six months because of the seasonal aspect of his business. That was all he wanted to hear. I brought him over to our commercial business department and he was set up with a checking account right away.

"Because my needs-focused approach of asking revealing questions and really listening to the answers was so unlike that of other banks he'd visited to 'just gather some information,' we not only got his commercial business, but he has since done business with our investment service department as well."

Bonnie Keller, Assistant Regional Manager of Central National Bank in upstate New York, tells a similar story. "A primary focus of my job is business development, one source of which is referrals from realtors," she says. "One particular realtor proved especially resistant to sending us referrals. My discussions with him as to why never moved beyond the point that, in his view, our products were not competitive, but he wouldn't say more.

"After participating in the Partner Selling program, which emphasizes getting to the bottom of the prospect's concerns with probing questions and not just trying to *sell* all the time, I realized I hadn't been dealing with this prospect correctly. I arranged another appointment to explore his mindset by asking open-ended questions and truly listening this time.

"After a short period, I could see an immediate difference in how we communicated as evidenced by the type of information he was revealing. Among the things he told me was that the types of products and services we offered needed to be expanded and our turnaround time on mortgage approvals needed to be much faster. This was valuable information to me. I took it back to the bank, we changed our product offerings and shortened the time we took to process mortgages, and that realtor has been referring business to us ever since."

Revealing questions should begin with one of the following six words: What? When? Where? Why? How? Who?

If, for example, I ask a client-prospect, "Do you like the weather?" I will most likely get a brief yes or no response. But if I restructure my question to, "What is it about the weather you like?" I cause the person to elaborate, to reveal his or her feelings on the subject.

You should be very cognizant of asking questions that will result in a more revealing response, that will disclose more information, that will help you *probe* for an opportunity.

Next, these questions should be progressive in nature.

In other words, *they must lead somewhere*.

Follow-up questions should grow from previous ones in a straight line that will lead to a conclusion.

You begin at one side of the continuum asking low-risk, nonthreatening questions, then progress cautiously and methodically toward the high-risk area: the payoff questions designed to expose the opportunity or reveal that none exists.

Here's a list of general need-development questions, moving from low-risk to high-risk, to offer you an idea of how that progression should evolve:

What do you look for from a supplier?
Why are you looking for this?
What's been your experience with other vendors?
What happened then?
Were you satisfied with that?
What would you like to change?
What problems do you want to solve?
What would happen if the problem was corrected?
What kind of cost savings would you experience?
What is your time frame on this process?

What is your budget or price range?

At the end of this chapter, there are some blank pages for you to design some general need-development questions of your own.

Write yours and mine directly into your pre-plan.

This will enable you to memorize them so that your need-development questions will be on the tip of your tongue.

You will not be groping for them when you get face-to-face.

Your Need-Development Questions

POINTS TO REMEMBER:

- Prepare your need-development questions ahead of time.
- Get the prospect to do 80 percent of the talking.
- Design probing need-development questions.
- Begin with *what, when, where, why, how,* and *who.*
- Listen carefully and write down what you hear.
- Adjust pace to the prospect's personality style.
- Move progressively from low-risk to high-risk questions.
- Write them into your pre-plan.
- Memorize them.

CHAPTER EIGHT

Translating Value: The Bedrock of Sales Success

"Features alone do not always show value. The value must be revealed."

If an opportunity—a potential match for a win-win situation—has been uncovered during the needs-review, it is now the sales person's turn to do the talking.

At this point the sales person presents the product or service being offered and communicates how the product or service will address the client's specific needs and help the client achieve his or her specific goals.

This step is called *translating value*.

The Dual Priorities

Translating value has two components of equal importance.

The first is the *feature(s)* of the product or service being presented.

A "feature" can be defined as what there is about the product or service that is indisputable. In other words—the facts.

For example, the surface of my desk furniture is flat. Its flatness is a feature. That feature is indisputable.

The second component involved in translating value is the clearly stated *benefit* of the product or service feature.

For example, because the surface of my desk furniture is flat, it is convenient to work on. I can spread a lot of material out on it.

It's crucial to remember that the client may not always perceive the value of the feature from the feature itself.

The sales person must powerfully depict the value of his or her product/service for the client in terms the client can easily understand and appreciate.

Traditional selling typically lets the features speak for themselves.

Banks are a good example of the traditional approach.

Their brochures are loaded with features, usually described in the most esoteric banking industry terms and jargon. Things like FDIC, truncation banking, ATMs, and so on.

Clients look over these terms and shake their heads.

"What do they mean? What do they do? What's the benefit to *me*?"

The value of these features is seldom translated; instead it is concealed from the client mumbo-jumbo that intimidates rather than communicates.

The medical industry and physicians are also notorious for this practice.

Patients entering a hospital or doctor's office are inevitably full of fear. They wouldn't be there in the first place if there weren't something wrong with them, so they're frightened. "How bad is it?" One of their needs is to feel secure in the doctor's hands so they will be less frightened. Recognizing and meeting this need is something a doctor should be able to do.

One of the ways to do it is to communicate how the treatment to be undertaken will benefit the patient—in terms the patient can understand.

If a patient feels confused or intimidated by some complicated medical procedure, it is important for the physician to pick up on this and translate the value of the procedure in straightforward language so that the patient can perceive that value and feel safe and secure.

My father swears by his doctor. Loves him. Wouldn't think of going to anyone else. Why? Because the doctor takes the time to explain things to him in words he can understand, that are not intimidating. He responds to my father's need to feel he is in good, safe hands. They are partners in the relationship; my father feels it and that means value to him.

Point the Way

Any organization must understand that if clients are left to translate the value of a product or service feature on their own, they may not take that step.

Or if they do they may make an error in the translation.

They may misinterpret the benefit(s) you're trying to get across.

Misinterpretation can be worse than no interpretation.

It is therefore important for the sales person to do the translating—and to do it in clear, simple, and straightforward language—to make sure there is no room for error or misinterpretation.

There's a revealing story about Federal Express in this regard.

In the 1980s, Federal Express ran a series of television commercials promoting its vast fleet of 300 airplanes.

The spots showed aerial views of the Memphis, Tennessee Airport, the company's hub, and the giant fleet of 300 planes lined up on the tarmac.

What was being sold in these spots was the feature: the fleet of airplanes. This was the selling point, the message being "Look how big we are! We've got 300 planes!"

Through subsequent market analysis and advertising research, however, Federal Express discovered that, left to interpret the benefit—the value—of the feature of having such a large fleet on their own, people were reaching a very different conclusion than Federal Express expected and wanted.

People took a look at these commercials, at this huge fleet on the tarmac, and said, "I'll bet having all those planes costs FedEx a bundle to operate. It's probably a very expensive service to use."

People also felt that having such a huge number of planes increased the chances of their packages being lost, mislaid, and not getting to their destinations on time, or at all.

By stressing the first component of value translation, the feature, but ignoring the second, the benefit, Federal Express had left its message wide open for misinterpretation. And the company found itself dissatisfied about what its clients thought.

Federal Express has since corrected the mistake by clearly translating the value to the client of doing business with a company that has a fleet of 300 airplanes via its slogan: "When you absolutely, positively have to get it there." No room for misinterpretation there.

Features alone do not always show value. The value must be revealed.

Another story.

I was in the market for a swimming pool a few years ago.

The sales person approached me and immediately launched into a machine-gun-like presentation of all the features of the pool I happened to be standing next to and looking at, which, to him, obviously made the pool a must for me.

This guy really knew his stuff. I figured he'd just graduated from pool school because the pool's features and all the pool industry jargon imaginable just tripped from his tongue.

The trouble was, I didn't have the slightest idea what he was talking about.

He waved his hands excitedly and waxed rhapsodic about the pool's "extruded aluminum design."

"Excuse me," I said. "What's that?"

He gritted his teeth and kicked the wall of the pool with his foot—kicked it so hard I thought he hurt himself. But the wall of the pool didn't budge.

"I see," I said. "But why's that important?"

"So that in the winter when there's thousands of gallons of water in there turned to solid ice, the walls don't crack," he explained.

Finally, he had translated the value of the product feature for me—in terms I could clearly and vividly understand as well as appreciate.

I was sold on the value of an extruded aluminum design in a swimming pool.

But I had to drag the value out of him.

If I had been just a regular customer, I might not have bothered.

The Partner Selling approach doesn't leave this option open to chance.

Seems like common sense, doesn't it?

And yet it's surprising how little common sense many sales people show when they come to the critical step of defining the why and how—the benefit to the client—of what they're selling, not just the what.

Connecting Features to Benefits

The addition of several of the following transitional phrases to your Partner Selling vocabulary will force you to *always* translate value. Place these phrases between your features and benefits:

This allows you to . . .
Which means . . .
Therefore . . .

So you can . . .
The benefit, or value, to you is . . .

The more technical your product, the more useful these transitional phrases are.

For example, "This computer comes with extra memory; *this allows you* to store every important document you have."

Another example. "Our bank offers truncated checking accounts; *which means* all your canceled checks are stored here for your convenience *so you can* avoid cluttering up your home or business and won't risk misplacing or losing them."

These phrases compel you to connect the feature to the benefit, to move logically from one to the other, so that value is translated for the client in words he or she can understand.

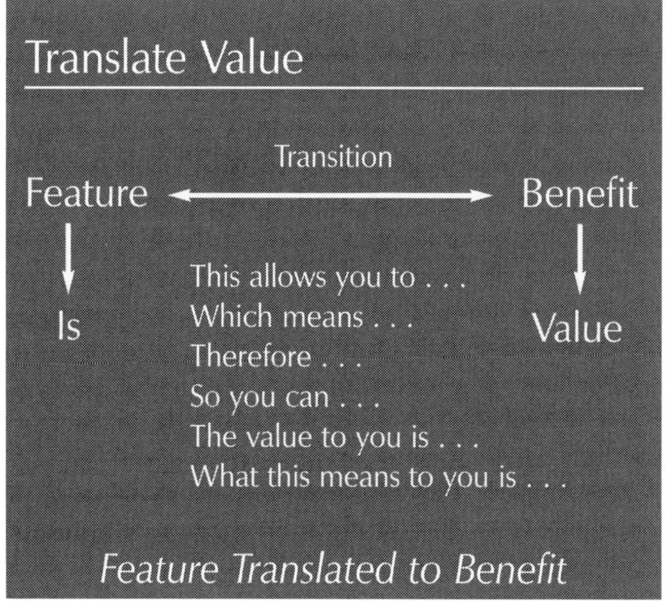

Use Testimonials

Third party recommendations or endorsements of your product or service assist enormously in translating value.

They lend credibility to your presentation by substantiating it.

If others have used your product or service, achieved measurable results, found doing business with you to be a pleasant and profitable experience, and are willing to say so, make sure your potential clients know about it.

You can't buy better value translation than this. Such endorsements or recommendations provide clear and impartial validation of the claims you are making, turning them into indisputable facts that your clients and prospects can neither ignore nor misinterpret.

The value translation of what you are offering becomes objectively apparent, and clients/prospects sell themselves—the primary goal of the Partner Selling approach!

Translating Value Counterattacks Commoditization

Oscar Wilde once described a cynic as a person who knows the price of everything and the value of nothing.

In this sense, most clients and prospects are cynics. Traditional selling has made them that way.

It all but *forces* clients to become price-conscious.

The end result is the commoditization of your product or service. The Partner Selling approach, emphasizing translated value, can help you avoid falling into this trap.

Computer stores are a good example of how not translating value in clear and understandable terms brings out the price-conscious cynicism in clients.

Most of the sales people you find selling computers are absolutely horrendous at translating value, at connecting the feature to the benefit. They seem totally locked into feature-consciousness.

I was in the market for a specific kind of laptop computer. I must have asked the sales person at the first store I went into to stop talking at least five times, to slow down, stow the features mumbo-jumbo, and explain to me in words I could grasp what benefits these features offered to a nonexpert like me.

He never did.

Ultimately my decision to buy or not to buy this computer came down to the best deal I could get. In other words, *price*.

The government is another good example—perhaps the best example—of how failure to translate value promotes price-conscious cynicism.

The government is terrible at translating the value of the programs and services it offers to "We, the People." I think this is the principal reason why many Americans believe their tax dollars are not being spent wisely.

By not translating value, the government encourages Americans to look at such programs and services as commodities—and people simply don't feel they're getting their money's worth.

The ability to translate value is the most important weapon in any organization's arsenal for avoiding this scenario.

People who feel they are getting their needs met, who feel a sense of receiving benefits —of achieving greater value— from the product or service being offered will focus on more than just price in making their decision.

The higher the price of the item being sold, the more critical translating value becomes as a method of counterattack.

This story told by Howard Katz, District Manager of Leviton Manufacturing, shows why translating value is such an important element of the Partner Selling process.

"One of our sales people has always believed that the option to match the other guy's price is a must-have for getting the sale, even though I have explained to him many times that we do not, and cannot, let the competition determine our price levels," Howard says. "This has generally led to a great deal of frustration on his part, feeling that it tied his hands.

"Recently he came to me about a potential sale again seeking approval to match the competitor's price. Again, I refused. But this time, having gone through the Partner Selling program, I was able to point him in a more positive direction.

"Convinced his hands were no longer tied, he went to the customer and outlined the many value-added services we brought to our customers in general that would be of benefit to this customer in particular which our lower-priced competitors were unable, or unwilling, to provide.

"The following week I received a copy of an invoice from him showing that he had gotten the order at our price. His note on the invoice read, 'Thanks to Partner Selling.'"

Vincent Gandolfo of Frank Crystal Benefits, a New York City insurance company and client of the Partner Selling

Group, reinforces this approach. "As a manager of 20 professional insurance consultants working with mid-sized employers, I continue to see favorable results from the 'translate value' component of the Partner Selling equation," he notes. "Many of our new business successes in the past year were a direct result of differentiating the value *we* bring to the table as insurance brokers/consultants from that of our better known competition. Here's an example:

"A big private school with about 150 full-time faculty and staff needed to make a decision about which medical insurance company and broker to go with. Even though our stiffest competition had a premier reputation and greater name recognition in the marketplace, which the school had decided would be the primary focus in making its decision, our account executive was able to shift the discussion to a more value-oriented focus during his presentation," Vince says.

"By clearly conveying how the products and services we brought to the customer's table made us different, and persuasively illustrating what these distinctions *meant* to the customer in real terms, we were selected to be the school's new insurance broker instead of our higher profile competitor. In fact, the school now relies on us to negotiate all its business and accomplish all of its objectives in the insurance arena."

Partner Selling sales people must be able to establish the "*value proposition*" with their clients. That is to say, they must position themselves as being *more valuable* than the products or services they provide. You can accomplish this by using the Partner Selling model.

Know When to Stop Talking

The danger exists that value can be overtranslated.

As important as it is for the sales person to do most of the talking during this step, it is equally important for the sales person to recognize at what point he or she should stop talking.

A good rule of thumb is: *Give clients and prospects just enough value information for them to convince themselves to buy.*

How do you know when you have accomplished this—when enough is enough and that it's time to move on to negotiating?

As you translate value, your client or prospect will be giving off "buying signals."

These are indicators of how the value information you have imparted is being received—favorably, unfavorably, or somewhere in between.

It is extremely important to recognize buying signals and comprehend their meaning.

These signals, or indicators, can be very subtle, or quite overt. They can be verbal and/or nonverbal.

For example, if the client leans forward, nodding his or her head as you talk, this indicates interest—that what you are saying is getting through and making a positive impression.

If the client's expression remains impassive throughout the presentation, this may indicate lack of interest, some feeling of reservation about, or a buying objection to, the product or service you are offering that may impede making a decision.

If clients begin to ask questions that show that they already see themselves owning your product or taking advantage of the benefits of your service—such as "How long will it take me to get up to speed?"—you should interpret it as a positive signal that they're ready to move forward, to negotiate. Their acceptance of the feature/benefit connection that you've demonstrated to them is a great indication that they want you to move forward with them.

POINTS TO REMEMBER:

- Establish what features about your product or service you're going to present based on the client's needs.
- Identify the appropriate benefit or value of those features for the client.
- Eliminate or clearly explain jargon that is industry-specific.
- Use transitional phrases like those suggested above to connect features to benefits.
- Use testimonials that include measurable results to substantiate the value of your product or service.
- Recognize when it's time to stop talking and move to the next step.

CHAPTER NINE

Negotiating as a Partner

"Initiate the closing step—and involve the client in exploring solutions to possible objections."

Reaching a Mutual Agreement

What often happens after sales people have made their presentation and are about to enter the negotiating phase of the interaction is that they suddenly stop.

They're worried about being too aggressive, of being rejected if they push for a decision. So, they freeze up.

They reason, "Think it over while I step out for a cup of coffee. Call me when you are ready."

They wait for the client to take the next step.

In Partner Selling, the sales person always initiates the closing step that can bring up points of negotiation.

Buying Signals

By paying close attention to "buying signals," initiation of the closing step can be accomplished without creating unnecessary pressure on the client or the sales person.

Buying signals must be observed very, very carefully.

They point the way to the next step in the Partner Selling process—easing into the negotiation, or closing action.

Some clients show buying signals more openly than others.

Expressives, for example, give off lots of buying signals.

Analyzers on the other hand are much more reluctant; it's difficult to get a handle on what they're thinking.

Some clients are very experienced at *not* giving off buying signals, regardless of their personality type.

In fact, some companies send their purchasing agents to school to learn how to be totally nondescript in word and gesture when the sales person is making the presentation.

Ask Trial Close Questions

Trial close questions enable the sales person to move toward an appropriate closing action without fear of putting a lot of pressure on the client to make a decision and therefore risk the possibility of being rejected.

Trial close questions are especially important in the absence of buying signals.

If you have absolutely no idea as to how your client or prospect is reacting to your presentation, where he or she may or may not be in the buying process, asking some trial close questions can shed the necessary light.

Trial close questions are designed to elicit an *opinion* from the client, not push for a decision.

Their purpose is to help you determine where the client or prospect is in the buying process without making the ultimate decision to buy or not to buy.

As a result, trial close questions should be relatively low key to avoid the appearance of sales pressure—even though pressure is what forces a decision.

Just like the questions you asked in your needs-review stage with the client or prospect, trial close questions should move along a continuum, starting with relaxed and easy (i.e. nonaggressive, completely nonthreatening) questions and then increasing to more aggressive (i.e., more probing) trial close questions.

Deciding where you should begin your questioning along the continuum depends on the client/prospect's personality type.

With a Dominator, you can get straight to the heart of the matter in your trial close questioning (the far end of the continuum).

With a Steady or an Analyzer personality type, you should proceed more slowly and cautiously. Start out with simple

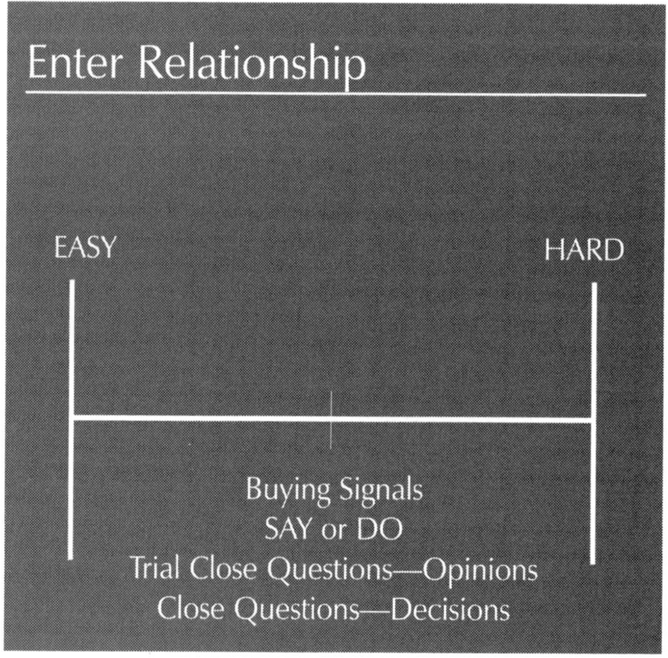

questions that call for a simple response. Then ease into a more pointed and aggressive line of trial close questioning that will gradually lead to more complex (i.e., insightful) responses.

A good example of relaxed and easy-going trial close questions (the left end of the continuum) would be:

"How does all this sound to you?"
"What do you think of what I've presented to you so far?"

These are very low-pressure questions that ask for a general opinion. They ask for a feeling, not a decision.

As we move to the middle of the continuum, we come to a more probing type of trial close—the either/or question.

These questions are aimed at gently nudging the client forward by providing him or her with two *positive* options from which to choose. Some examples:

> *"Would you like to do this on Tuesday, or would Thursday be more convenient?"*
> *"Is your goal to start in April, or would May be more realistic and effective for you?"*
> *"Do you like the red model, or is the blue more attractive to you?"*
> *"Is paying in cash agreeable, or would you prefer some other terms?"*

Trial close questions which fall at the far end of the continuum are more aggressive and probing because they are specifically aimed at eliciting a response that will ask for a decision. Therefore, they are more direct. Some examples would be:

> *"Do you want to start this on Tuesday?"*
> *"How much of a deposit would you like to put down?"*
> *"Are you going to enroll all your people into this program?"*

From your trial close questions, you will get one of three responses: positive, negative, or neutral (i.e., indecisive).

A positive response to even the simplest trial close question instantly jumps the process forward. A deal may be struck then and there.

A negative response indicates an obstacle in the path toward negotiation.

It reveals that an objection exists in the client's mind that must be dealt with before you can proceed.

A negative response alerts you to the need to regroup.

It also determines how aggressive and probing you must be with your next line of closing questions.

By its very nature, a neutral response to a trial close is evasive. It tells you nothing, or at most very little, about the client's feelings.

Evasive, neutral answers show the client or prospect is stuck in place. You want to structure your trial close questions in such a way as to call for concrete responses, whether they be positive or negative.

Dealing with Objections.

The late, great golf teacher Harvey Penick tells a story in *The Little Red Book* about a "New Yorker," a high-handicap golfer, who came into Penick's pro shop one day.

"You're Harvey Penick, aren't you?" the man asked.

"Yes."

"I understand you're the best golf instructor in America."

"Well, I don't know about that," Harvey said humbly.

"Can you teach me how to get out of sand traps?"

"Sure," Harvey answered. "Follow me."

The two of them walked out of the pro shop and Harvey took the man directly to the driving range, ignoring the sand area altogether.

"Wait a minute," the man said, glancing at the sand area they'd walked right by. "I thought I asked you to teach me how to get out of sand traps?"

Harvey looked at him and said, "First let me teach you how not to get into them."

Partner Selling operates on the same principle.

It positions the sales person to anticipate potential problems or objections to the sale during the needs-review.

In this way, the sales person will have a strategy for dealing with those problems or objections when they come up during the negotiating phase, which is where they typically arise.

Objections fall into four categories:

Price—the client thinks it will break the budget.
Product—the client isn't convinced it will do the job.
Procrastination—the client wants to put off making a decision.
Personal—the client has taken a dislike to the sales person.

Dealing with these objections is a two-step process.

The first step is to define the actual problem, and the second step is to fix it.

Step one is critical because it involves finding out if the prospect is being straight with you.

Is the prospect telling you the truth about the problem or objection he or she has—or masking the real issue by telling you something else?

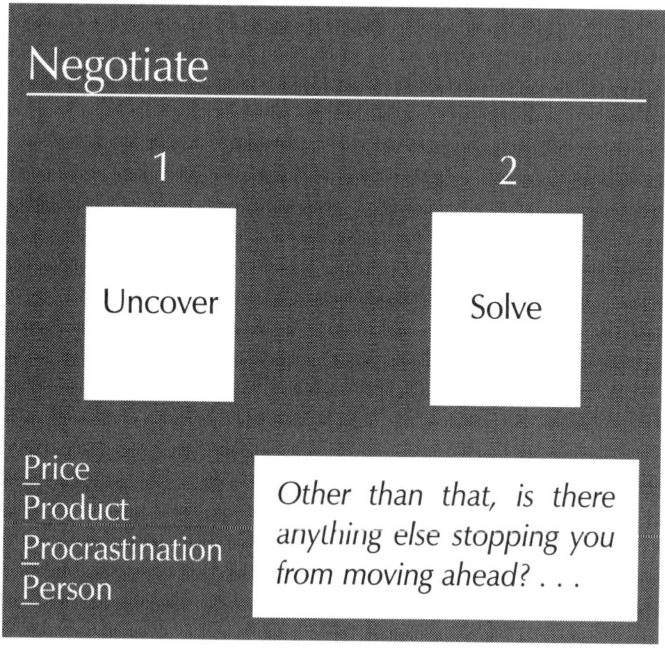

For example, a client or prospect may *say* your product or service is the problem, but deep down he or she isn't persuaded it will do the job, or that the solution it provides will respond to his or her needs.

Or, the actual problem may be the price of the product or service, but the prospect is hesitant to say so for some reason.

Perhaps the prospect feels there is no room to negotiate on price and masks this assumption by objecting on other grounds like the product or service itself.

At this point if you accept what the prospect says at face value and attempt to fix the product/service problem when the real issue is the price, you immediately lose control of the negotiation.

In other words, fixing the wrong problem has the same effect as not fixing the problem at all.

So, before you can attempt to fix the problem the client or prospect has stated, you must first determine whether it's the real one.

To get at the truth about a negative response, you have to ask another trial close question or a series of trial close questions designed to isolate the objection.

If, for example, the client or prospect indicates the problem is the product, you may say, "Okay, let's put that aside for a moment. Apart from that issue, is there anything else that you feel might be a problem?"

If the response is "no," then you've most likely identified the genuine problem and can attempt to fix it.

If the client scratches his or her head and says, "Well, now that you mention it, the product really suits my needs, but I'm not sure if I can afford it," your isolation of the objection has now led to the exposure of a real obstacle. You've gotten the truth and therefore you can proceed accordingly.

By using this approach, you get the client or prospect to genuinely partner with you in exploring possible solutions.

Personal objections are the most difficult to overcome because they are typically the most concealed.

Very seldom will a client or prospect look you in the eye and say, "The reason I don't want to buy your product or service is because I don't like you." The objection will either be attributed to one of the other Ps—price, product, or procrastination—or it will be left unstated. The client or prospect simply shuts the door.

I used to buy all of my golf equipment at a particular sporting goods store. But I stopped doing business there when, on two separate occasions, I witnessed the owner yelling at one of his employees—a young kid—rebuking and embarrassing him right in front of me and other customers.

The way he treated that kid—and, judging from this example, probably the rest of his employees as well—was awful. It left a bad taste in my mouth. I thought, "I don't want to do business with someone who treats his staff that way" and haven't been back to that store since. He lost my business but has no idea why because my objection was personal.

Most customers may feel the same way in a similar situation.

If their objection is personal, they will either not say what their objection is or they may cover up what they are thinking by making up something to say.

Now that you've isolated and identified the real problem, how do you proceed to step two—fixing the problem?

There are several ways.

If, for example, price is the real issue, you can lower your price or lose the sale. Or, you can rereview the client's needs and retranslate your product's value so that it's clearer to the client why your price is justified.

All too often, the untrained sales person lowers the price too quickly if this objection is raised, thereby diluting—perhaps even negating—the entire value translation process.

When this occurs, clients or prospects may be left with a feeling of unease and mistrust.

They begin to think along these lines: "You've just gotten through translating the greater value of your product for me, telling me how much more it's going to add to my life, and now you're willing to cut price at the drop of a hat?"

The subtle message is that the sales person has exaggerated or distorted the value of the product and that it really *doesn't* justify the price because it's not worth what the sales person says it is.

Trust and rapport go out the window—possibly so does the sale itself. The potential for entering into a long-term, mutually beneficial partnering relationship with that client could be jeopardized.

Deflect Premature Price Questions

Companies sometimes lose sales because their sales people allow themselves to respond to price questions from clients or prospects too early in the process—before they've been able to establish the value of their product or service. Clients and prospects tend to ask questions about price early in the negotiation process. This is based upon their legitimate concerns.

As a sales person, you may want to deflect or avoid answering such questions before you have taken the time to fully demonstrate the value of the product or service you are offering.

The Partner Selling system can help you do this because it is designed to help you focus on selling the value of your product or service, not its price.

Perhaps your price can be duplicated elsewhere. However, there is tremendous value in doing business with someone who knows a great deal about the client's concerns, problems, and solutions. Therefore, the benefits of that client's entering into a relationship with you *cannot be duplicated*.

Deflecting premature price questions gives you time to powerfully drive this message home.

POINTS TO REMEMBER:

- Initiate closing. Don't wait for the client or prospect to do this.
- Ask trial close questions to find out where the client or prospect is in their buying process.
- Move from low-risk to high-risk closing questions.
- Confront objections.
- Isolate objections to smoke out the client's real problem.
- Respond to the right problem, not the wrong one.
- Deflect premature price questions to prevent your potential client from making a decision based on price rather than value.

CHAPTER TEN

Entering into a Relationship, Not Just Closing the Sale

"Relationship building is the link between buyer loyalty and supplier profitability."

Moving to the Next Step—Confirming the Beginning of a Relationship

The term "close" has been used in sales training classes for years as signifying the successful conclusion of negotiations.

I've used it myself throughout this book because it is the familiar term sales people tend to apply to their objective, the goal they are trying to achieve with the prospect or client they've approached.

But in today's selling environment, the way the term "close" has traditionally been used is inaccurate.

Closure is *not* what the dynamic new selling philosophies like Partner Selling teach or seek to accomplish between buyer and seller. Nor is closure what today's buyers want and expect from the vendors who supply them.

To close implies the shutting down of something that possibly may not be reopened; for example, when a company goes out of business it closes its doors—forever.

"Close" suggests the point at which something has been ended, wrapped up, or concluded. The finish line.

In Partner Selling, however, the term "close" is an action not a goal.

It is the action that leads to the goal.

It is not the shutting down of something, but the opening up, or beginning, of a long-term relationship, or union, between buyer and seller—a partnership.

The term "close" may still function appropriately as a description of the sales person's immediate short-term objective, the selling transaction. But in our context, "close" becomes the sales person's ultimate objective to enter into a relationship with the prospect that will add power and profit to both parties again and again.

John Giordano, President of Plaza Travel Center in upstate New York, is a longtime friend who has successfully grown his full service travel company by assisting businesses in the design of incentive travel programs for their customers. He was asked to consult with a window treatment manufacturer. The manufacturer, which had a great reputation with its customers as a quality company, wanted to build stronger relationships with a particular group of its better dealers.

This manufacturer has a bright staff of management officers and marketing people. John, by using his Partner Selling skills, succeeded in making them comfortable enough to share the sales strategy and financial information he needed in order to begin designing a program. He was then able to suggest a program that included desirable destinations at the right time of year, for the right number of people, offering the right kind of amenities appropriate to the program's theme, and also included full reservations for all attendees and advanced marketing promotion and on-site staff to run the trip—all within a realistic budget that enabled the manufacturer to achieve its bottom-line goals.

Furthermore, by clearly demonstrating that he was part of the team, John cemented a relationship with this manufacturer that promises additional opportunities for designing its travel incentive programs in the future.

The Partner Selling approach goes beyond the instant gratification of the here-and-now, one-time-only transaction. It strives to enter into a long-term relationship with the client or prospect by adding the new ideas and vitality businesses and industries desperately need if they are going to be successful.

As a goal, Partner Selling applies to every type of sales person at every level within any sales organization regardless of the product being sold.

For example, sales people in retail department stores wait on clients every day whom they most likely will never see again. In other words, they deal with customers on a short-term basis. But their long-term objective is to keep those customers coming back to the store—to enter into a relationship with the store based on the satisfaction of having their needs continually met by whoever waits on them.

Clients versus Customers

If you perceive your prospect as a potential *client* rather than a potential *customer*, your expectations for your relationship with them will be different and your attitude and your behavior towards them will also be different.

You will psychologically move toward the goal of entering into a relationship with them.

In the context of selling, the term "customer" means someone with whom you engage in a transaction—implying a short-term, perhaps one-time-only deal.

The word "client," which in the past has been used only to describe certain specific selling contexts, is now more appropriate for describing your "customers" in today's new selling environment.

Why?

Because the word "client" suggests an extension beyond the short-term or one-time-only transaction to an ongoing relationship.

As companies navigate their way through the choppy waters of unprecedented global competition into the next century, more and more of them are facing up to the fact that those to whom they supply products and services want to be viewed and treated as clients, rather than customers.

The changes occurring in the banking industry are indicative of this new reality.

In the past, banks were not especially relationship-oriented.

If a person walked into a bank to make a deposit, the transaction was over until the next time a deposit was made. It was assumed by the bank that the person would come back. After all, where else would he or she go?

Under siege from investment firms, financial planners, and a host of other competitors and technologies with whom and through whom people like you and I can do our financial business, banks have now realized that only by developing relationships with their clientele can they keep that clientele coming back to them and using their services.

This is especially true of the future lifeblood of any industry or business—younger generation consumers—who have so many options available to them (i.e., at-home personal computers, etc.) to do their banking and investing.

If a bank doesn't meet any of their product or service needs, they can and will go elsewhere for less cost.

Banks are responding to this by becoming more customer-friendly—by treating customers like clients, the way an investment firm or financial planner does.

Relationship building has become a life and death issue for banks and many other industries and businesses today.

It is *the* link between buyer loyalty and supplier profitability—the link that Partner Selling can bridge.

POINTS TO REMEMBER:

- Create a relationship mindset by viewing prospects as clients, not customers.
- Look upon the "close" as the beginning, not the end, of the relationship.
- Aim for a long-term partnership based on a mutual win-win relationship.

CHAPTER ELEVEN

Sales Management the Partner Selling Way

"The ability not just to survive but succeed in today's ultra-competitive world demands from sales people a high degree of personal mastery."

Qualities of an Effective Partner Selling Sales Manager

The role of the sales manager is going through a dramatic shift in today's business environment. It's no longer the same job it was in the past. And in the future, it will likely continue to evolve into a job that makes a real difference in the performance of sales people.

I believe this evolution in the sales manager's role, when understood and embraced, will have a significant, measurable, and positive impact not only on sales people but on the sales culture at large, as well.

Today's new-generation sales manager must be able to do a far greater number of things than their predecessors had to in order to perform their job well. For example, they must be able to:

Organize themselves and others.
Run *effective* sales meetings.
Evaluate sales training.
Evaluate, diagnose, and treat negative sales behavior.
Make effective presentations.
Be familiar and at ease with each advanced new selling technique and technology and share know-how.
Understand what motivates sales people.
Enhance product knowledge.
Understand and be a whiz at compensation issues.
Efficiently manage time and territories.
Deal with senior management.
Balance the needs of sales people with the goals and expectations of senior management.

My client and friend Tom Jordan, National Sales Manager for MBIA of Armonk, New York, puts it this way: "My biggest challenge in managing the twenty or so sales people I'm responsible for all over the United States is dealing with so many different personalities. Knowing what makes my sales people tick and how to move them to their next level of effectiveness is an ongoing demand. I have to be a psychologist, a friend, a nurturer, a trainer, and a cheerleader all at once, while, at the same time, keeping my eye on the bottom line as sales manager in order to achieve the company's desired and expected results."

This is a very tall order to fill indeed, one that is made particularly difficult due to the lack of preparedness many sales managers have for lack of training.

Most sales managers I work with came up from the selling ranks where, typically, they were such excellent performers that at some point they caught the eye of senior management who promoted them out of those ranks into the position of sales manager, a job they had little, if any, training or preparation to assume.

What happened then is a prime example of Professor Lawrence Peter's so-called "Peter Principle." Many of them soon discovered that the skills they had developed, which made them such great sales people, were very different from those required to become equally great sales managers, especially these days. As a result, they were not as effective in their new role as they had been in their old one.

Lack of the skills needed to do such a different job had, in the parlance of Professor Peter's "Principle," led to their being promoted to a "level of incompetence."

What makes this situation doubly frustrating for those suddenly thrust into such a precarious position is that there are few, if any, avenues for them to explore to get the help, guidance, and training they need. *The reason is that identifying and developing the skills required to meet the changing responsibilities of today's new-generation sales manager is a subject about which very little has been written.*

The next time you go into a bookstore, take a look at all those shelves bursting with books on the climatic changes today's new selling environment is undergoing, and on the new selling techniques and strategies authors and experts have come up with to address them. The scarcity of contemporary literature on the sales manager's changing role in this new business environment and of training guides and other self-help resources for today's new-generation sales managers is positively astonishing.

The Link to Increased Sales

Because today's well-educated clients and customers *expect* more from those with whom they do business, seeking relationship-oriented partners rather than dollar-sign-oriented order-takers, sales managers are now being challenged to move away from the traditional role of monitoring and evaluating the performance of their respective reports "by the numbers"—i.e., by how many sales calls they make in a month. Sales managers have to become builders and developers of the skills their sales people need to deliver more. They must be prime motivators who possess not only a deep understanding of what it takes to move sales people to higher levels of performance but who have the ability to *inspire* sales people to achieve those levels. As a result, their position has become *the* vital link in the company chain of command in terms of producing and generating increased sales.

Sales managers who perform these functions well have thus become very valuable partners to all concerned—to the company that employs them, to the internal customers (sales people) they're responsible for, and to the external client or customer whom they ultimately serve and with whom sales people must forge ongoing relationships that achieve win-win results.

I expect the partnering value of the sales manager function will only increase as we enter the next millennium and the demand for ever-greater productivity in the face of ever-stiffer global competition increases as well.

As amorphous as its responsibilities may seem and as daunting as it may appear, this new-era job really boils down to some very straightforward tasks the sales manager must be able to perform well.

Let's take a look at each one, and how to develop and hone your skills at them the Partner Selling way.

Inclusive Planning

The days of the sales manager who just comes up with quotas and arbitrarily tells sales people to "Go out and produce or else," or who hopes sales people will get excited about and committed to achieving some despotically concocted list of expectations are over.

Today's sales managers must be more inclusive about drawing their sales people into the sales planning process and in defining their sales objectives as a group.

They must understand how to get their sales people more *involved* in this process and possess the skills necessary to get them to buy into achieving the defined objectives at a greater level of enthusiasm and commitment than ever before.

In effect, today's sales managers must become less quota-oriented and more goal-oriented, for the reason that a quota is something that someone else sets for the sales person, whereas a goal, or objective, is something the sales person actively participates in setting for him- or herself and therefore has more of a personal stake in wanting to achieve.

Inclusive sales planning requires establishing a mutually arrived at plan of action with specific, clearly stated, and prioritized goals and objectives, then periodically re-evaluating that action plan and reprioritizing as necessary to reflect current realities. It's just common sense to involve sales people in this process, since they are the ones who will ultimately have to carry out the plan of action and thus need to support it completely in their hearts and minds.

Whether you decide to gather all your people together in the conference room for a group sales meeting, or work with them one-on-one, here's what I recommend to invite greater participation and achieve better results.

The Partner Selling Sales Management Planning System

Create a Mission Statement.

This specific and positive statement should address what it is you are trying to achieve with the product or service you offer, or what your department or company seeks to achieve—in others words, its *purpose.* It should extend beyond the obvious mission of just making a profit. The mission statement requires only a couple of sentences to lay things out. If you have clearly defined your purpose, your statement will be sharply focused, thus brief and to the point. This purpose, or mission, can be short-term or long-term. As most companies already have an existing mission statement, review it carefully to make sure your department's mission statement is in sync and not in conflict with the company's. If your respective mission statements are at odds with each other in some sense, an obvious need for a meeting of the minds has presented itself in order to resolve the disparity with company management, *whose own statement of mission may, in fact, turn out to be the culprit, the one that requires rethinking and retooling.* If your company doesn't have an existing mission statement, this is an excellent opportunity for you to help create one for it from the ground up with the help and participation of the very troops who will be carrying it out. For example, here's the Partner Selling Group's mission statement:

"To provide sales organizations and sales people with training programs, key note speeches, and learning systems that cause them to examine and continually improve the way they sell and serve their clients."

List the Critical Issues.

The reason it is so important to have a participatory discussion with your sales people about the creation or re-evaluation of your department's mission statement is that it forces close examination of all the critical issues that will impact the mission's being successfully achieved. Many of these issues will change as you address them or deem them less important. List and prioritize these issues and publish them so that *everyone* in your department or company will get a "heads-up." Some broad categories of critical issues impacting a company or department's ability to carry out and achieve its mission statement might be:

- Electronic commerce
- Employee hours
- Marketing
- Product development
- Sales budgets
- Sales forecasting
- Training and development

Be specific and put some meat on the bones of those broad categories of critical issues, however. For example, here are some of the nitty-gritty critical issues John and I have identified as requiring attention so that the Partner Selling Group will be able to carry out its stated mission:

- Hire a new marketing assistant.
- Create a new preview video.
- Revise and update this book for the publisher.
- Update the group's Web site.

Attach Goals and Objectives to Critical Issues.

Now it's time to narrow your focus even more by moving from a broad statement of your mission and what the critical issues are that will impact achievement of that mission to setting your goals and objectives with regard to each of these critical issues, one by one. Goals and objectives are precise statements of what you intend to do, and when, to tackle each issue. In other words, they are a feasible means of meeting the particular issue head-on. In order to be as precise as possible, apply the S-M-A-R-T criteria to each critical issue in developing your goals and objectives. Ask yourself, are your stated goals and objectives you've established for meeting that issue:

S*pecific?*
M*easurable?*
A*ttainable?*
R*ealistic?*
T*rackable?*

Let me give you an example. One of the critical issues we've identified in the Partner Selling Group's mission statement is to hire a new marketing assistant. Here are the goals and objectives we established to address this critical issue using the S-M-A-R-T criteria:

Critical Issue #1: Hire New Marketing Assistant — S-M-A-R-T Goals and Objectives:

- Place newspaper ads by February 5th.
- Establish compensation plan by February 15th.
- Interview five candidates by February 26th.
- Make decision by March 5th.
- Have new-hire on board by April 2nd.

Simply put, your goals and objectives are targeted plans of action—and practical time tables for implementing and achieving them—attached to each larger critical issue that you and your sales people have identified as requiring group focus and effort in order to fulfill your department's more sweeping purpose and sales action plan.

Self-Management Is a Must

I cannot tell you the value I place on being my own boss, of not having to report constantly to some supervisor to tell me what to do, how to do it, and when.

I *love* having that freedom.

But in order to preserve it, I have to be able to manage myself, my time, and every aspect of my business effectively. Because if I don't, or even if I just slip up occasionally, I stand the chance of not only losing my cherished freedom, but my business and my livelihood along with it.

Next to running your own business, sales is the one job I can think of that offers the opportunity for such autonomy almost intrinsically—which, as I noted in the previous chapter, is why many people who like working on their own are drawn to sales as a profession in the first place.

But this autonomy presents a big challenge. The ability to *function* autonomously, not to mention preserve one's autonomy by being successful, demands from sales people a high degree of personal mastery.

Sales people must be extremely well organized. They must use their available time to maximum advantage in *every* business situation. They must continually position themselves to spend the right amount of time and effort on the right—i.e., the most rewarding and productive—*kinds* of activities. They must be technologically proficient—i.e., able to use the latest automated tools for doing business more efficiently. They must manage their sales territories well, which means being able to determine the appropriate frequency for seeing prospects and clients so as to achieve maximum penetration and impact in their respective markets.

Sales people who do not possess these qualities and skills innately, or who do not strive to develop them, are not only bound to fail in preserving what autonomy they have in their respective selling environments, but are probably destined to find themselves in search of a different line of work in fairly short order. In today's ultracompetitive selling environment where sales managers are spread so thin by so many other new and demanding responsibilities that they can ill afford to micromanage their sales team even if so inclined, the ability of the sales person to manage him- or herself has become *an absolute requirement of the job!*

Today's new technologies for conducting business can help sales people better manage their time and their territories (see Appendix II). But unless they're in firm control of their own *behavior* first, no amount of timesaving automated technology will ever prove sufficient.

Good self-managers not only stand a better chance of surviving in today's ultra-competitive world, but are better able to capitalize on the Partner Selling process to a much greater degree than those lacking in self-management skills, thereby achieving something more than just survival: Selling Success.

The quest for newer, more efficient methods of managing their time and territories more effectively is, or should be, a never-ending one for sales people because there is no one-size-fits-all perfect final solution to this ongoing problem. As we move into a new century of global competition unparalleled in our experience, this quest will become even more critical as the demands and stresses placed on sales people to conquer time step up in ways we can't even begin to imagine now.

Following are some techniques and strategies I use with clients to get them truly focused on the important issue of how to sharpen their time and territory management skills.

Evaluate Your Strengths and Weaknesses

Before seeking ways to hone *any* skill, it only makes sense to determine what your skill level is *now.* Otherwise you won't know how much honing is required, or where it should be applied.

How good a self-manager are you? Take a few minutes to complete the following self-evaluation.

Partner Selling Personal Diagnostic Test

Answer each of these questions by putting a check mark in the appropriate blank. When you're finished, give yourself 4 points for every "Often" checked, 2 points for every "Sometimes" checked, and 0 points for every "Rarely" checked. Then add them up to see how you stand as an effective time and territory self-manager.

	Often	*Sometimes*	*Rarely*
Do you handle each piece of paperwork just once?	( )	( )	( )
Do you begin and finish projects on time?	( )	( )	( )
Do people know the best time(s) to reach you?	( )	( )	( )
Do you do something *everyday* that moves you closer to achieving your long-range goals?	( )	( )	( )
When you are interrupted, can you pick up where you left off without losing momentum?	( )	( )	( )
Can you deal politely yet effectively with long-winded callers?	( )	( )	( )
Do you focus on *preventing* problems rather than dealing with them after they occur?	( )	( )	( )
Do you meet deadlines with time to spare?	( )	( )	( )
Are you on time to meetings, to work, and to events?	( )	( )	( )
Do you delegate well?	( )	( )	( )
Do you write daily "To-Do" lists?	( )	( )	( )
Do you finish all the items on your "To-Do" list?"	( )	( )	( )
Do you update, in writing, your professional and personal goals?	( )	( )	( )
Is your desk clean and organized?	( )	( )	( )

Can you easily find items in your files?	( ) ( ) ( )
Do you use time-management tools, such as voice mail, e-mail, pager, contact management software, an opportunity manager, conference planner, and time analyzer?	( ) ( ) ( )
Have you broken your accounts down by territory in prioritized A, B, C fashion, and established a sales call frequency for each?	( ) ( ) ( )
Do you spend sufficient time exploring opportunities for entering into new business relationships?	( ) ( ) ( )
Do you currently apply any of the steps in the Partner Selling process to managing your clients and prospects?	( ) ( ) ( )
Are you able to focus on high-payoff selling activities and not get distracted?	( ) ( ) ( )
SUBTOTAL	_ _ _
	x4 x2 x0
TOTAL	_ _ _

Total Points

- 49–80 You're an excellent manager of time in consistent control of your days.
- 37–48 You manage time well but need to be more consistent.
- 25–36 You are too often a victim of time, where the days manage you rather than the other way around.
- 13–24 You are perilously close to losing control of your time, and you need to get your priorities straight.
- 0–12 You've completely lost control of your time, are overwhelmed, scattered, frustrated, and probably under a lot of stress. Take immediate, remedial action or you could be history.

Know Your Enemies

If your score on the diagnostic test was low, it's clear that something is preventing you from managing your time effectively. In fact, experience tells me there is probably more than one thing preventing you.

I call these obstacles "time robbers" because that's exactly what they do. They steal precious minutes and hours from you every day, sapping your energy and your capacity to function productively, always leaving you behind the eightball—*mainly because you let them!*

Before you can overcome these obstacles and turn your behavior around, you must first know what they are. Identify them by reviewing the following list and placing a check mark in the blank next to every thief that's robbing you of precious time.

( ) Poor Planning
( ) Meetings
( ) Failure to Listen
( ) Lack of Authority
( ) Unclear Goal(s)
( ) Waiting for Answers
( ) Socializing
( ) Interruptions
( ) Lack of Self-Discipline
( ) Shifting Priorities
( ) Unrealistic Time Estimates
( ) Poor Communication
( ) Your Own Mistakes
( ) Indecision
( ) Red Tape
( ) Procrastination
( ) Conflicting Priorities
( ) Cluttered Workspace
( ) Equipment Failure
( ) Lack of Motivation
( ) Lack of Procedures
( ) Negative Attitude
( ) Unwanted Mail/E-Mail
( ) Civic Activities
( ) Low Company Morale
( ) Others' Mistakes

( ) Peer Demands
( ) Lack of Delegation
( ) Unwillingness to Say "No"
( ) Overinvolvement with Details
( ) Other

____

____

____

Prioritize Activities Based on What Your Time Is Worth

How obvious this seems, yet how often we fail to do it, spending valuable time we can ill afford to lose on activities that yield so little reward.

The classic example of this is the guy earning $100 an hour who takes two hours out of his busy day to mow the lawn when he could get the kid up the street to do it for $10. He's not saving money. He's *losing* it.

Unless you know how much your time is worth, it's almost impossible to set your priorities correctly, since priorities vary not just daily but sometimes hour-by-hour. For example, should you be prospecting now? Servicing an existing account? Enhancing your product knowledge?

How Much Your Time Is Worth

The chart below of broad annual incomes shows what your time is worth, based on 244 eight-hour working days per year (assuming a five-day work week less vacation and holidays):

If Your Annual Earnings Are:	Every Hour Is Worth:
$10,000	$5.12
$12,000	$6.15
$15,000	$7.68
$18,000	$9.22
$20,000	$10.25
$25,000	$12.81
$30,000	$15.37
$35,000	$17.93
$40,000	$20.49
$50,000	$25.61
$60,000	$30.74
$75,000	$38.42
$100,000	$51.23

Now that you know how much your time is worth, you'll be able to assign a priority rating to all of the various activities in which you are engaged. Some things you do are more important, therefore more profitable, than others. Below, list the six most important things you do in descending order of importance (number one being most important). Focus your valuable time on these higher payoff activities from now on.

____

____

____

____

____

Prioritize the Kinds of Time You Need

A recent study showed that sales people spend an average of 15 percent of their work week in face-to-face contact with clients and prospects—a top priority on any sales person's activity list. If they could raise that figure by just 5 percent, look at how much more they would be increasing their opportunities for success.

Every activity requires other *kinds* of time in order to perform it more effectively.

For example, one week you may need more phone time for prospecting. The following week you may need more paperwork time for planning. And the next, you may need more travel time for going face-to-face with clients and prospects in various locations.

The key is to develop a sense of awareness of what *other kinds* of time you need, which will let you know instinctively where you may be falling short.

List the kinds, or blocks, of time you need and the percentage spent in each that will enable you to perform your key activities more efficiently and effectively on a week-to-week basis.

Kinds of Time Needed %

____

____

____

____

____

____

Prioritize Your Clients

Having taken the previous steps to look more closely at yourself and how you manage your time, now turn your attention to your clients—i.e., your territory—and take an equally close look at how you manage them in terms of time spent.

Territories are split up in various ways. For example, a sales person may be responsible for the whole state of Wisconsin, whereas another may have responsibility for the entire Northeast region of the United States. A territory may also be split up vertically, which is to say by industry category.

Regardless of how territories are split up, the common denominator between them is that each territory contains a subuniverse of clients with whom the sales person must deal on a regular basis.

The question is: *how regularly*?

And the answer is: *it depends*.

The nice thing about clients is that they're quantifiable. Typically, they break down along the following lines:

15 percent of your clients produce 65 percent of your total sales/gross profits. These are your "A" accounts.
20 percent of your clients produce 20 percent of your total sales/gross profits. These are your "B" accounts.
65 percent of your clients produce 15 percent of your total sales/gross profits. These are your "C" accounts.

Prioritizing them in such a manner forces you immediately to see what percentage of time—and at what frequency, or regular basis—you should spend in front of each group.

For example, if your "A" accounts produce 65 percent of your profits, it stands to reason that you should spend roughly the same percentage of time focusing on that particular group, even though it is the smallest one. And by breaking your A, B, C account lists down further still in terms of individual contribution to the whole, you have in front of you a road map that tells you how regularly you should be seeing each separate client.

Clip out and use the following territory management worksheet to identify your A, B, and C accounts and prioritize clients within each category (number one being the largest producer in the group, and so on). Add more lines as needed:

Territory Management Worksheet

"A" Accounts:	"B" Accounts:	"C" Accounts:
1. ________	1. ________	1. ________
2. ________	2. ________	2. ________
3. ________	3. ________	3. ________
4. ________	4. ________	4. ________
5. ________	5. ________	5. ________
6. ________	6. ________	6. ________
7. ________	7. ________	7. ________
8. ________	8. ________	8. ________

Time Analysis Worksheet for Sales Managers

HOURS		Comments
AM 7		
AM 8		
AM 9		
AM 10		
AM 11		
NOON 12		
PM 1		
PM 2		
PM 3		
PM 4		
PM 5		
PM 6		
TOTAL		

Record time use at least every hour. Draw a vertical line through time blocks occupied by a particular activity.

MONITOR YOUR TIME

It's all well and good to prioritize your most important activities, the kinds of time you need to perform them, and how frequently you should be seeing your A, B, and C list clients. But without monitoring how you *actually* spend your time—i.e., analyzing your real-world behavior—all of the above will be for nothing.

Many sales people don't do this because they simply don't know how. Let me show you a way that works very well with my clients.

Using the Partner Selling Time Analysis Worksheet, take the time blocks you identified earlier and write them across the top in the diagonal spaces provided. Then record at least every hour what time you spent in each block performing a given activity throughout a particular day. At the end of that day, or, better yet the following morning when you're fresh, look back at the sheet to see how you fared.

This exercise will provide you with precise feedback in a visual form about how much time you actually do spend in each respective area so that you can determine what changes may be in order to increase your effectiveness in reaching your priority targets.

PRIORITIZE YOUR "TO-DO'S"

Every sales person I know makes out "To-Do" lists to avoid forgetting any of the multiplicity of individual items they must deal with or tasks they must perform every single day. The trouble is, they usually make out these "To-Do's" in scattershot fashion, jumbling everything together in a way that

To-Do List

Do List for (Date)________________________

Priority Number	These items are urgent. I will do them without fail today. Priority numbers indicate order of work	Priority A, B, or C	Completing these items will help me reach my goals. Priority A items are most important.

offers no visual cues or distinguishing marks separating the more important "To-Do's" from the less important.

The result, more often than not, is that some important "To-Do's" get left out in the cold unattended to because many back-burner items have gotten taken care of first.

Let's face it, all "To-Do's" are not alike. Some are more critical or urgent than others. It's imperative to break them down.

The Partner Selling "To-Do" list gives you the opportunity, indeed forces you, to prioritize your "To-Do's" in such a way as to ensure that your most urgent work items are always taken care of and your most important goals are always reached first.

It involves assigning a number to each work-related "To-Do" that measures the degree of urgency (number one being the most urgent) so that you can lay down the precise order in which your "To-Do's" should be taken care of. Check each item off as completed, and, presto, you've got a written record telling you it's been done.

Additionally, assign a priority A, B, or C rating to each goal-related "To-Do," and follow the same procedure. In this way, you'll know that you've taken the proper steps in the right sequence for reaching your most important goals first.

Following the format shown in the worksheet, make out a Partner Selling "To-Do" list every working day, and you'll always stay on top of things.

Stay Focused

How often have you suddenly remembered something you needed to discuss with your company's financial services

Conference Planner

INSTRUCTIONS:
In the spaces below enter the names of those with whom you have frequent conferences. Jot down items you need to discuss with each. When the timing is right for a conference – by meeting or by phone – handle all items. Work on avoiding one- or two-item conferences.

NAME	NAME	NAME
NAME	**NAME**	**NAME**

or customer service people and dropped everything to deal with it there and then, or grabbed the phone and called a customer about an issue that suddenly came up and gotten involved in a lengthy conversation that throws your entire day off? This happens to every sales person.

Nothing can toss a monkey wrench into the most well-organized time and territory management plan more quickly than giving in to such situations.

Inevitably, there are people, internal and external customers alike, with whom you have frequent dealings on a variety of issues in the course of your day or week, ranging from items that pop up suddenly but are not emergencies to matters of routine.

To avoid falling into the trap of being constantly interrupted or distracted by such dealings, it's important to plan for them so that you always stay focused. The Partner Selling Conference Planner will help you achieve this.

Enter the names of those people with whom you have frequent dealings in the spaces provided. Jot down the five, six, or more items you must take up with each person. Then, when the timing is right for a conference (face-to-face or by phone), handle *all* of these items at once; avoid having just one- or two-item conferences.

You can enter the information manually onto a piece of paper or electronically into your laptop or desktop computer. However you choose to do it, use the format shown in the Partner Selling Conference Planner.

Run More Effective Sales Meetings

Sales meetings are an excellent vehicle for continually reinforcing the Partner Selling process or any other training program you've put in place to reach your sales objectives.

These meetings should be upbeat, motivational, and most critically, *highly interactive.* They should not be forums where the sales manager stands at the front of the room before the troops acting as a lecturer, barking pearls of wisdom and orders at them like a marine drill instructor.

A good sales meeting is a two-way street, involving the exchange of information and experience by *everyone* in attendance. As sales manager/coach, your main function is to keep the meeting moving on schedule according to the agenda you've developed and, most important, *focused on the subject under discussion*.

To reinforce the idea that the meeting is important, and thus important to attend, establish a climate for both starting and stopping on time. If everyone isn't there yet, start anyway. One of my clients pushes this to perhaps eccentric extremes, but his results have been effective. He schedules his sales meetings for Monday morning at nine o'clock, and promptly shuts and locks the door at that hour. If a sales person hasn't arrived yet, he or she is out of luck and not allowed in. This may seem a bit drastic, but it positively communicates the message that these meetings are important and that it's not a good idea for sales people to miss them. The proof is in the pudding: Nobody does get locked out because everyone makes sure to get there on time.

It's just as important to conclude the meeting when you said you would as it is to start on time. This not only enhances your credibility, but stopping on the dot may create a positive feeling of anticipation—in effect, make your sales people "hungry for more." If you don't get to something on your agenda during the meeting, table it until next time; never run over.

When done correctly and on a consistent basis, sales meetings can accomplish the following:

- Create a positive atmosphere for improving sales performance.
- Strengthen commitment to building client relationships.
- Encourage achievement of sales goals.
- Enhance product knowledge.
- Generate prospect and client development strategies.
- Provide an ideal environment for recognizing sales performance.

Develop an Agenda

The main purpose of a sales meeting is to have an excellent reason for calling it in the first place; otherwise it's just another exercise in eating up time. Your agenda should be straightforward and to the point, a simple, one-page outline of "when," "where," and "what" distributed to sales people when the meeting begins or, better yet, in advance of it so they can adequately prepare for the meeting and commit themselves to the agenda.

Once the meeting begins, and everyone has a copy of the agenda, briefly run through it so that everyone is clear as to how things will proceed.

Your agenda sheet should be set up in an easy-to-read and understand format (see sample at the end of this section) that provides or covers the following:

Logistical information—the date, time (i.e., 9–10 A.M.), and location of the meeting.

Top performer information—acknowledgment of individuals whose actions and results warrant singling out. This should always be done at the beginning of the meeting in order to start things out on a positive note.

Old business—review (and acceptance, if appropriate) of the record, or minutes of what transpired at the last meeting in order to identify what items may now be due or which actions still need to be taken.

New business—initial presentation of all current business developments, new items and issues to be discussed, and who will chair the discussion.

Strategic information—presentation and dissemination of information regarding new sales enhancement products, training programs and systems, self-development tools or exercises, and strategies sales people should know about and take advantage of. This part of the meeting is an excellent opportunity for stimulating more group interaction and exchange of ideas. For example, start off by having one of your top performers talk about the strategies and techniques he or she is using to achieve results with specific prospects and clients, then act as moderator for a group in bringing up additional suggestions and techniques.

Ancillary information—the passing along of additional "For Your Information" (FYI) items or activities sales people should be aware of that may be of interest and of possible value to them. This information should not be open for discussion during the meeting.

Adjournment information—scheduling of the date, time, and location of the next meeting.

Promote Participation

Once the meeting has been called and the agenda set, proper facilitation of the meeting itself is critical in ensuring its success.

The sales manager/coach must be able to move things along while not appearing to take over, and continually urge as much participation as possible while keeping everyone on track and on task in order to fulfill the meeting's purpose.

Opening the meeting is the responsibility of the sales manager/coach. But in order to set a participatory tone, he or she should begin involving people as soon as this is done. That's another reason why I suggest recognizing the super performers among the group for their achievements at the top of the agenda. It encourages involvement early on.

Here are some others ways to promote participation:

Sample Agenda Sheet Format

Name of Company

Sales Meeting Agenda

Date of Meeting: ____________________________

Time: ____________________________

Location: ____________________________

Recognition of performance: ____________________

Review of Old Business: ____________________

____

____

Discussion of New Business:

Topic: ____________________________

Time: ____________________________

Person: ____________________________

Sales Training & Development: ____________________

F.Y.I. ____________________________

____

Next Meeting:

Date: ____________________________

Time: ____________________________

Location: ____________________________

Ask open-ended questions. This challenges people to not only come up with ideas but think through them. Begin such questions with words like "what," "when," "where," "why," "who," and "how."

Engage people in decision-making. Instead of coming up with solutions to problems or issues that are raised during the meeting yourself, encourage people to interact, discuss, come up with solutions or potential solutions, and effect decisions themselves.

Avoid being judgmental. Refrain from asking people for their input and ideas, then arbitrarily shooting them down.

Listen. If you do all the talking and no one else can get a word in, you won't be exercising one of the most important skills a sales manager/coach must possess: actively making an effort to give others a hearing and *absorbing* what they have to say.

Give and encourage feedback. Sales meetings are a great opportunity for the sales manager/coach to get issues out on the table or to present new ideas and stimulate an immediate, honest response, whether positive or negative. To accomplish this, however, the sales manager/coach must give people sufficient time to express their feelings, and not react to them prematurely.

Take "Outcome-Oriented" Minutes

"Outcome" minutes are not the ordinary type of minutes usually taken down during the course of a meeting that simply provide a written record or summary of every word that's been said.

"Outcome" minutes highlight *action items*, the key issues that must be followed up on or key information that must be gathered in order to achieve a specific result.

Dos and Don'ts of an Effective Sales Meeting

Do	*Don't*
Allow for individual differences.	Allow late arrivals.
Be respectful.	Arrive late yourself.
Demonstrate enthusiasm.	Bluff.
Maintain good eye contact.	Ignore anyone.
Seek feedback.	Minimize the meeting's purpose.
Set positive example.	Ridicule anyone.
Show empathy.	Talk down to anyone.
Stimulate ideas.	Talk down your expectations.
Take personal interest.	Use sarcasm.

They should include identification of the person responsible for the follow-up or getting the information, the due date, and the outcome, or expectation, desired.

The following illustration shows you how to capture such minutes in an "Outcome" style.

Barriers to an Effective Sales Meeting

- Interruptions
- Lack of feedback
- Lack of organization
- Late arrivals
- Minimal group participation
- Noise

POINTS TO REMEMBER:

- Sales people who are unable to prioritize and remain disorganized are bound to fail as we move into an ultracompetitive new century.
- Without first changing your *behavior* to fix the problem, no amount of hot organizing tips, new selling techniques, or technological tools will help. Seeking ways to maximize your use of time and penetration of your territory is a never-ending process.
- Sales people who are skilled self-managers will be better able to reap the benefits of the Partner Selling process than those who are not.

CHAPTER TWELVE

Motivating and Coaching Partner Sellers

"Today's new-generation sales managers must move away from being performance monitors and evaluators and become more planning- and coaching-oriented—masters of the art of building and developing the skills of their sales people."

Motivating Sales People

Motivation is perhaps one of the most frequently used words in today's business arena. Employers are constantly seeking new ways to get their employees to work harder and smarter, produce more, and grow the bottom line.

The Partner Selling sales manager must not only contemplate the issue of motivation every day, but actively work to create an environment within the sales organization where the word is put into practice, becoming a living, breathing reality *every single day*.

The most obvious answer to what motivates sales people, or anyone else, is, of course, M-O-N-E-Y. It's a no-brainer. People work to make money so they can buy the things they need and want in order to live comfortably and securely. Therefore it's not surprising that most studies conducted to find what motivates workers reveal that money is very high on the list.

But usually there is only so much money a company or sales manager is able to throw around as an incentive for sales people to reach new heights.

What else can be used to positively impact performance?

THE MOTIVATORS

The psychologist Abraham Maslow (1908–1970) has identified a wealth of factors that motivate human beings, and has ranked them in order of necessity to the human psyche. He called this ranking a "Hierarchy of Needs." Each of these needs, which range from basics like food and shelter all the way up to ego-gratification, requires satisfaction and fulfillment before the person can seek to achieve the next item on the list.

Drawing upon Maslow's "Hierarchy," let's explore what else motivates sales people—and, implicitly, what Partner Selling sales managers can use as motivators to create an environment where sales people keep pushing themselves to achieve their personal best.

Accountability.

Sales people are fully aware of the important role they play in the success or failure of any departmental project or objective. They know that if they fail to deliver, they will be held accountable for their failure. There's a flip side to this. They also want to know that if they succeed they will be held equally accountable for that too and receive credit when credit is due. They want to know that they won't have their thunder stolen out from under them by some credit-hogging manager, or anyone else. Give credit to others on a continuous basis, where and when appropriate.

Achievable Goals.

Sales people need to have a sense that they *can* win. What is expected of them individually or as part of the team—whether it's the number of new prospects to be targeted each month or the volume of sales to be reached—must not be so high as to be unattainable regardless of how much effort they put in.

Acknowledgment.

A sales person, like anyone else, enjoys receiving a pat on the back for a job well done, especially in front of his or her peers. It makes the person feel like a "star." By offering such recognition and appreciation, you send a clear message that good performance is not taken for granted, which makes the person want to do even better and get more "Atta boys." By expressing the message in public, you ensure that word gets around.

Authority.

Sales people need to believe they have both a fair amount of power to make decisions on behalf of the company and the responsibility to do so vis-à-vis their clients and prospects, particularly during the negotiating phase of the selling process. If they have neither, their feelings of authority and strength in such situations are undercut. They shouldn't have to come running to you, the sales manager, whenever things get down to the nitty-gritty. Such a lack of authority shows that you have little faith in their abilities or judgment and it reflects badly on them with the customer.

Availability of Training.

Knowing that the company is committed to offering assistance to raise their skill levels through ongoing programs or classes in everything from product knowledge enhancement and selling strategies to time management is a very important motivator. It makes sales people see the value in striving to become more effective. Moreover, it shows that the company truly is behind them and dedicated to their future growth and advancement.

Competitiveness.

By competitiveness I mean the internal spirit that naturally exists on a friendly basis among coworkers in any organization to outperform or beat the other guy. Encourage it.

Confidence.

Sales people like to work in an atmosphere of freedom where they are allowed to function autonomously and don't have someone watching over their shoulders or breathing down their necks, monitoring their every move. By promising such autonomy, you show your sales people that you have confidence in their ability to manage their own time effectively and that you put your faith in them to do so. Don't renege on that promise, or *any* promise for that matter. Otherwise you'll lose the return confidence and faith you've inspired in them to make them strive to meet your expectations.

Income Potential.

Sales people have a big advantage over folks in other professions in that they typically work on a salary plus commission basis, an arrangement whereby there is a direct correlation between how well they perform and how much they can earn. Depending upon the company, industry, or type of customer sold to, the percentage breakdown can be as widespread as 20 percent salary/80 percent commission. The higher the cap, or ceiling, in their earnings potential, the better many sales people like it, and the more this can be used as a motivator, because "the sky's the limit."

Job Security.

The days of "a job for life" are gone. And good riddance, for they were contrary to the goal of striving to reach ever-higher plateaus of performance and achievement. Nevertheless, in these days of mergers, acquisitions, and corporate downsizing, sales people want to know that if they do work harder and smarter and continuously exceed expectations, that they won't be vulnerable to some general, across-the-board employee cutback stemming from one or all of the above. A company's soundness, financial and otherwise, historically and in the foreseeable future, and, most important, its *word* are strong incentives for attracting and keeping good sales people, and a key motivational issue.

Nurturing Environment.

By showing that you like, appreciate, and support them, value their efforts, are an ally in their empowerment of *themselves* to prosper, you foster an environment where the sales person's feelings of admiration for others and self-esteem are constantly being nurtured and reinforced. Sales people *thrive* in such an environment.

Participation.

By being given the opportunity to put their two cents' worth in on what goals should be set and how best to reach them, sales people assume a degree of ownership in the game plan. This serves as a mighty motivator for them to do their utmost in winning the game.

Pride of Accomplishment.

Conviction that they really have achieved something significant, either individually or as a group, is a big time motivator for sales people. For example, one of my clients, Howard Katz of Leviton Manufacturing, was recently notified that his district, one of 13 within the company, was up 13.6 percent in sales that month, the highest increase over any other district. When I congratulated him, I mistakenly referred to the figure as 13.5 percent. "No! It was 13.6 percent!" he corrected me. Though I was just a tenth of a percent off, the *exact figure* meant a great deal because that was the achievement he and his district were being hailed for, and its specificity was important to him. He was so proud of this accomplishment that he was highly motivated to repeat, if not exceed it next time, and to continue to be the leader among his district peers.

Quality Products.

Like everyone, sales people want assurance that they're getting the best value for their money in the purchases they make—that what they're buying isn't subquality, that it's reliable, and, if it's to be delivered, that it will get to them on time. It only stands to reason that that same assurance about the product they're selling will enable them to sell that product with greater confidence and conviction and achieve better results. A good quality product made by a reputable firm backed by dependable service that provides genuine value to the customer is one of the strongest motivators a sales person can have.

Self-Worth.

People like to see themselves as winners. Winning anything, whether it's the lottery or a simple door prize, reinforces and enhances a good self-image. Holding contests and giving out prizes or awards—a nice lunch, an expensive dinner, an exotic trip, a plaque, whatever—stimulates an atmosphere of excitement within the sales organization. It gives sales people a valuable extra to shoot for, which they have a reasonable chance of winning (unlike the lottery) and can feel good about for having won.

Square Deals.

Sales people are not inclined to go the extra mile for a sales manager who treats them unfairly or rules them with an iron fist. Being constantly browbeaten to "perform," and made to accept whatever is dished out with a smile because they're "lucky to have a job" are sure recipes for resentment, resistance, and subpar results. By the same token, if they do happen to do something wrong or their numbers do slip from time to time, sales people want to feel confident that this too will be dealt with fairly and squarely by the sales manager.

Upward Mobility.

If they perform like cream, sales people expect to be able to rise to the top, or at least have the chance to do so. Can they become district sales manager, regional sales manager, or perhaps even a vice-president of the company someday? Promotional opportunities are a strong catalyst for drawing good people and a powerful motivator for getting the best from them.

Variation.

Repetition of the same tasks year-round or having the same goals to achieve from month to month makes sales people stale results-getters at best and at worst turns them into clock-watching zombies. Sales people require a continuous challenge—whether it's being given a different type of customer to deal with as a change of pace, a new product to sell, or a new service offering to promote within their existing product mix—to keep them motivated to perform at their best.

(For additional perspective on the role of the new-generation sales manager "from the field" in today's Partner Selling environment, see Appendix I.)

SOME TELL-TALE SIGNS OF A MOTIVATIONAL PROBLEM

Lack of Attendance.

The sales person is frequently "out sick," consistently tardy for meetings, late for appointments with customers and prospects or misses them altogether, and avoids spending time in his or her territory.

Lack of Energy.

The sales person seldom comes up with ideas, exhibits little excitement or enthusiasm, and appears totally uninvolved. This is a definite sign that the selling environment itself is anemic and needs a motivational transfusion.

Lack of Positive Attitude.

The sales person thwarts his or her efforts from the get-go by taking the position that the sales plan is no good or that it won't work in his or her territory because that territory "is different from anybody else's."

Lack of Satisfaction.

The sales person is in constant complaint mode, always whining about one thing or another—the product's no good, the territory's lousy, his or her customers are "the bottom of the barrel."

Lack of Resistance.

Instead of bitching all the time, which at least shows spirit, the sales person never complains or puts up a fight about anything. He or she adopts the passive role of "yes man."

Lack of Time.

The sales person consistently fails to meet goals, objectives, and expectations that have been mutually agreed upon because "There just aren't enough hours in the day." This is a sure sign of poor self-discipline.

The Partner Selling Sales Management Coaching Intervention System

Since today's sales managers have to be motivators rather than dictators, they have to learn to conduct frequent individual coaching sessions with their sales people to keep or get them moving in the right direction.

Coaching requires a high level of skill, especially if, as is most often the case, the need for the session is due to a behavior problem the sales person has developed that is impeding his or her job performance and impacting the effectiveness of the department as a whole.

Such confrontations can be sticky indeed. Sales managers must be able to address a negative topic in a positive way. They must be able to get the sales person to recognize the existence of the problem and agree on its specific nature. Then the sales person must buy into a solution and game plan for correcting the problem and, ultimately, turn the situation around so as to achieve a win-win outcome for everybody.

This is an extremely difficult task to perform. It is only human to try to avoid doing it for as long as possible. By that time, intervention may be too late. If the sales manager keeps putting the coaching session off, or conducts it unsystematically and on-the-fly, the sales person's negative behavior is either never addressed or never fully corrected. Each of these scenarios leads to even *more* difficulties for the sales person, the sales manager, and the department, a lose-lose situation all the way around.

Whether you, as a sales manager, are intervening to help an already productive sales person reach the next level, or to help a problematic sales person turn things around, effective coaching boils down to a systematic, straightforward process. The bottom line is to coach with specific goals in mind. Here's how the Partner Selling Sales Management Coaching Intervention System does it.

Create a Safe Environment

Blind-siding a sales person by collaring him or her in the hallway for a quick, impromptu conversation about a performance issue, or suddenly bringing that issue up in a public setting where the sales person's coworkers can see and hear everything are sure ways of making the sales person feel insecure, threatened, hostile, resistant, and inclined to just "clam up."

Therefore, your first order of business is to nourish an atmosphere that allows the sales person to feel at ease, comfortable, willing to let his or her hair down, and talk freely and openly with you.

State the Time, Place, and Location of Meeting in Advance.

Schedule a specific time for the coaching session that is mutually convenient, arrange a specific location that ensures complete privacy, and, most important, tell the person what the meeting is generally going to be about ahead of time. Leaving the sales person entirely in the dark as to why you want to see him or her is guaranteed to get the session started off on the wrong foot. It causes the sales person to speculate unnecessarily ("What have I done?"), worry unduly ("What's going to happen to me?"), and show up feeling so gun-shy, tense, and uncommunicative that the session's failure is all but foreordained.

Build Rapport.

Start the session out on a positive note by reassuring the sales person that the conversation you are about to have is not going to be harmful, and is not intended to be a slap on the hand.

Avoid Interruptions.

Close the door to discourage intruders, shut off your cell phone, and if the location is your office, instruct your secretary to hold all calls and appointments for the duration of the session. There is nothing more annoying or guaranteed to make the sales person feel insignificant and conclude that you're just offering lip-service than repeatedly being "stranded in limbo" as you take every call and respond to every person who barges into the room.

EXPLORE THE ISSUE

You've already notified the sales person what the general topic under discussion will be. Now you want the person to open up and express his or her own views and opinions on the topic. You want to move gradually toward a more pointed discussion of the particular issue that needs to be resolved, remaining on an equal footing.

In other words, what you're trying to do here is make the sales person talk, to gather information *from his or her point of view* that will gain both of you a deeper understanding of the situation. You must get the person to come to his or her own realization that there *is* a problem and recognize the specific issue that's causing it (the person may, in fact, be "clueless").

Ask Revealing Questions.

Be pointed and direct, but not pushy or confrontational. For example, let's say the person's productivity is down and the issue is that he or she hasn't been making sufficient sales calls each month. Draw the person into exposing the issue and putting it out on the table him- or herself by asking such questions as:

"How are things going?"
"Why does there seem to be a discrepancy between how well you say things are going and the sales results I'm seeing from you?"
"What's your thinking on the sales results you've been achieving?"
"What do you think is causing your low productivity?"
"What can I do to help you understand the problem?"

Actively listen to answers. Hear what the person is saying and acknowledge this.

Guard Against "Deflecting" Comments.

If the person isn't "clueless" about the existence of a problem, he or she may try to divert your attention away from it by bringing up other, perhaps unrelated, issues or problems. Keep your eye on the ball and don't allow the person whose behavior is being discussed to stray from the subject at hand.

Make Strong Eye Contact.

Look directly at the individual at all times. Avoid letting your eyes drift and giving the impression that you're uninterested or inattentive to what he or she has to say.

Let the Person Finish Before You Respond.

People hate to have others jump in before they finish talking. I know I do. It makes me feel that they're either not really interested in what I have to say, or that they consider what they have to say is more important.

INTERVENE

Up to now you've sought to remain an objective participant in the process, but if the issue is not yet out on the table in the way it needs to be for the coaching session to move to the resolution stage, it's time to assume a more aggressive role in order to get the sales person off the dime.

Define the Issue Clearly.

Get right to the heart of the matter by telling the sales person in plain, unambiguous language what you perceive the issue to be. Example: "Your volume of sales this quarter has fallen sharply below that of the previous quarter, and so has the number of sales calls you made to clients and prospects."

Give Details.

Following on what you just said, explain what you mean by offering data. Example: "Results show a 20 percent decline in sales over the previous quarter and a drop-off in sales calls to clients and prospects of about the same percentage."

Use statements like:

"It appears that there may be a connection between the two."
"While listening to you, I get the feeling that you're unaware of this."
"Tell me about your relationship with Client X."
"Your numbers/behavior indicate that you seem to be having some difficulty achieving results lately."
"How do you react to what I'm saying to you?"
"How do you feel about your results not being what they need to be?"

Focus on the Issue, Not the Person.

Even if you're really angry with the sales person about the situation, remember and reinforce the idea that the issue is the problem, not the individual, that the negative here is not directed against him or her as a person. Emphasize that he or she has proven to be a very capable performer in the past and can be again, provided the real negative here, the *issue,* is successfully resolved.

Identify the Obstacles.

Now that the issue (i.e., decreased productivity stemming from a shortfall in sales calls) is squarely on the table, you want to move toward overcoming it. Before this can be done, however, some final probing is needed. You must smoke out the particular barriers the sales person is encountering, which gave rise to the issue in the first place. They have to be broken down or broken through so that a successful outcome can be achieved. For example, perhaps the sales person is suddenly experiencing difficulties managing his or her time or territory effectively, which had previously not been a problem. What are the roadblocks now being encountered that hadn't been in his or her path before? List them.

SUMMARIZE AND TAKE ACTION

Now you're ready to move toward a resolution that will (hopefully) correct the performance problem. Clip out and use the *Partner Selling Coaching Summary Form* included at the end of this section to facilitate this final stage of your coaching session. It will ensure that both of you are in complete sync about everything that's been covered, what direction you're headed in with it, and when you intend to get there.

Ask the Person to Summarize What He or She Has Gotten Out of the Discussion.

This serves to expose any misunderstandings on the sales person's part that could impede his or her progress or lead to additional problems or disputes later on. It gives you the opportunity to straighten things out right away and proceed on course.

Agree on Actions to Be Taken and Outcome.

Discuss and spell out the means by which the sales person can remove the obstacles that are impeding his or her performance. Make clear the specific steps the sales person should take to improve, communicate your expectations, and mutually agree on the outcome that is to be achieved.

Schedule the Next Coaching Session for Assessing Progress.

Establish a timetable for improvement. As it typically takes thirty days to make or break a habit, this is a reasonable length of time for the person to turn things around. Of course, a longer timetable may be necessary, depending upon the nature of the issue and difficulties of the obstacles that must be removed. Again, seek agreement. You're partners in this, remember. Then set a date to get together again for a follow-up coaching session to assess the sales person's progress, or lack thereof, in resolving the issue.

Partner Selling
Sales Management Coaching Intervention Process

1. Create a Safe Environment:
   - a. State purpose of coaching session
   - b. Value the person
   - c. Build rapport
   - d. Reassure the person
   - e. Plan an uninterrupted session
   - f. Begin a two-way dialogue
2. Explore the Issue:
   - a. Ask questions that are:
     - ■ Focused ■ Brief ■ Clear ■ Open-ended
   - b. Ask what and why questions, such as:
     - ■ "What can I do to . . ."
     - ■ "What is your thinking on . . ."
     - ■ "What will happen, if . . ."
     - ■ "What I am hearing is . . . is that right?"
     - ■ "What do you think caused . . ."
     - ■ "It is still not clear to me. What would happen if . . ."
     - ■ "What can we do to . . ."
     - ■ "Why do I have a sense that . . ."
     - ■ "How do you feel about . . ."
     - ■ "Why is there a difference between . . ."
   - c. Guard against "deflecting" comments
   - d. Active Listening Skills:
     - ■ Good eye contact
     - ■ Take notes
     - ■ Tune the world out and the person in
     - ■ Let the person finish before responding
3. Intervention Process:
   - a. Define the issue clearly
   - b. Begin intervention with some of the following statements:
     - ■ "It appears that . . ."
     - ■ "Your behavior shows . . ."
     - ■ "I have a sense that . . ."
     - ■ "While listening to you . . ."
     - ■ "Tell me about . . ."
     - ■ "Before you go on, do you mean that . . ."
     - ■ "I didn't understand that last comment . . ."
     - ■ "I'm having a problem with . . ."
     - ■ "I'm very concerned about . . ."
     - ■ "Your productivity has . . ."
   - c. Center on issue, not personality
   - d. Identify the obstacles
4. Coaching Summary:
   - a. Ask person to summarize discussion
   - b. Both agree and write down specifics on worksheet
   - c. Identify date and time of next coaching session
   - d. Follow up and monitor results/improvements

POINTS TO REMEMBER:

- Effective sales management is a powerful weapon in a company's arsenal for increasing sales through a more productive workforce.
- Today's new-generation sales manager must possess a diversity of skills to perform this difficult job well.
- They must be a combination of expert planner, psychologist, cheerleader, coach, friend, and nurturer, while also serving as buffer with senior management and keeping an eye on the bottom line.
- Create a motivational environment that constantly challenges your people and drives them to improve their selling skills.
- Involve sales people in the sales planning process of defining the mission, the critical issues impacting the mission, and the goals and objectives required to successfully carry out the mission.
- Evaluate, diagnose, and treat negative sales behavior that prevents a subpar performer from becoming a super producer.
- Partner with sales people (internal customers) the same way they partner with clients (external customers) in building trust, rapport, and lasting, win-win relationships.

APPENDIX I

The Sales Manager as Partner: A View from the Field

Mark Fitzgerald has been a friend and colleague of mine for fifteen years. Of the many sales managers I've known and worked with, he is the most gifted at creating a business environment that produces and develops successful sales people.

Mark's ability to understand the needs of those in his charge and to provide for them a model working environment that allows them to develop is remarkable. He has successfully coached sales people to become high-income producers.

I've watched Mark accomplish this as sales manager at four different companies throughout his career—several times against great adversity.

Mark has witnessed all the changes that have occurred in selling over the past quarter century and has been using

Partner Selling for more than ten years, training his people to build relationships with clients.

"It all gets down to uncovering the client's problem and being able to relate the solution back to the problem through the benefit your product or service offers," he says. "Being organized, disciplined, and a self-starter are the key elements in navigating that circle successfully. Partner Selling can help sales people do that. In effect, it trains them to be their own sales manager."

I sat down with Mark and asked him to share his ideas on how he brings about such successful selling results.

MARK FITZGERALD: I've always broken selling down into two parts. The first is the technical side of sales; the other is the personal side.

The technical side involves learning how to take the sale through a series of steps so that it becomes a logical sequence of events. Then you can track where you've been, where you are, and where you're going in each sale.

In fact, while on a sales call with one of my sales people it hit me how much I use the Partner Selling method to do this.

I work with many sales people, and I find myself entering the sale at a different point each time I make a sales call with one of them. And I use the Partner Selling method to identify what that point is. Is the sale on course? What hasn't been done? What needs to be done? It gives me great versatility and confidence.

Let me share an experience with you. One of my sales people, Dianne, brought me along on her third sales call to a customer that had been doing business with us forever. We were in the "Translating Value" stage, of demonstrating our equipment, when the customer informed us she was going to get competitive quotes. Dianne was floored. She thought we were the only supplier being considered. What had happened? I began to ask some questions and found that because of our long-standing relationship with the customer, Dianne had taken a lot for granted in the "Reviewing Needs" stage of the sale. I quickly backed up and started asking some need-development questions. The customer responded quickly, and 15 minutes later the sale was back on track. Our product was clearly the right one for the customer and we closed the deal that day. The customer was happy. We got the sale. And Dianne, once again realizing the value of a sales process, vowed never to take anything for granted ever again.

BOB FRARE: That says it all, doesn't it? Tell us about the personal side.

MARK FITZGERALD: The personal side of selling is made up of confidence, motivation, and a positive attitude. With all the competition they must go up against today, sales people need a high level of confidence and motivation. If they fall below that level, they need to get it back, be it through motivational books, tapes, and videos, selling techniques like yours, their sales manager, networking, or all of the above.

BOB FRARE: And if they don't get it back, they're stuck?

MARK FITZGERALD: That's right. They lose their edge. Selling is a process of continual self-development. Every time someone has a major success story in sales, they tend to write a book about it. Maybe they've just developed a new perspective on prospecting. Whatever it is, you can learn, you can get better by listening to their experience. Sales people should consistently and progressively study the process of Sales and Marketing or they will be left behind. The information available to us is increasing dramatically, and sales people need to tap into that. New thoughts are constantly being driven into the marketplace—and they're changing our business at a feverish pace. Sales people who only try to please their managers or do only what their companies want them to do, who do not try to inform or develop themselves, are terribly handicapped today when they go up against the competition. A sales person pursuing success should read sales books, selling magazines, listen to sales and motivational tapes, attend seminars and training courses, and network with their colleagues for ideas constantly.

BOB FRARE: How can a sales manager provide the kind of motivational support a sales person needs and help the sales person become his or her own sales manager?

MARK FITZGERALD: The sales manager of the present and future must know how to develop and build his or her people, how to coach and strengthen them. Teach them how to do all the right things consistent with adult business behavior. Genuinely motivate them to be happy, to *like* what they're doing. If you're in the selling game and you're competing against a sales person who's happy, motivated, confident, and well trained, and you're lacking in one of those areas, you'll be playing catch up. Good sales managers make a daily routine of having fun at what they're doing. It becomes infectious, and the productivity impact is enormous.

BOB FRARE: In what way?

MARK FITZGERALD: Happy sales people convey confidence when they go face-to-face with clients. That rolls over into the client and their willingness to do business. The negatively reinforced sales person, the one whose manager says, "Make your quota or you're gone," communicates very different vibes to the client—which gets in the way of their success. The carrot and stick approach of threatening the sales person to perform is outdated, outmoded, unproductive, and unprofitable. Smart companies and sales managers concentrate on training and motivation. They set realistic quotas and prepare the sales force to be confident, informed, and easy to do business with.

BOB FRARE: In other words, you've created an atmosphere that is all positive—and that produces incredible results.

MARK FITZGERALD: Yes. Our sales people consistently outperform the competition. Most of our competitors would like to come to work for our company. We're concerned about the person. We do everything we can to make and keep our people happy about our company, about their job, and that produces enormous victories.

BOB FRARE: In your view, where does account strategy fall: on the technical side or the personal side of the selling equation?

MARK FITZGERALD: The technical side. In order to become their own sales manager, sales people need to develop a system to track where they've been, what they're doing, and where they're going with each client or prospect. What is your next step? It's a major focus in sales today. If you don't have a system to keep track of that, the next step won't happen. A sales person should track their progress on a daily basis—because moving each account from step to step occurs on a daily basis. There are several computer software programs available to help the sales person do that. We use ACT! contact management software. It focuses on the contact, the relationship the sales person has with the client over a long period of time so that the account can be effectively managed.

BOB FRARE: What's the purpose of tracking?

MARK FITZGERALD: To set goals and enable you to look back each week, month, or year to see if you're meeting them. Tracking is really an issue of discipline and balance. About doing things that need to be done every day in order to reach goals sales people have set for themselves or their company has set for them.

BOB FRARE: What else does a sales person have to do every day to be their own sales manager?

MARK FITZGERALD: Sales people must be masters at managing time. They need paperwork time, computer time, personal development time, product knowledge development time. They need time for sales meetings. They need phone time with clients and prospects—and, of course, face-to-face client contact time. All these demands on their time mandate a great deal of time management skill.

Successful sales people manage their time very effectively, allotting the appropriate amount of time to each item for the results they seek to achieve. The higher the potential payoff for the item, the more time it should consume. The appropriate amount of time must be available for that item. Time management is how you make sure there is.

BOB FRARE: Do you mean spending more contact time on sales opportunities with potentially higher payoffs?

MARK FITZGERALD: Exactly. If you're in a quick-sell type of situation, you should be making twenty or thirty phone calls a day. If you're selling photocopiers, you should be contacting at least ten customers or prospects a day, and scheduling at least two face to face appointments a day. It's a numbers game. It's a balancing act. You have to be organized. Most sales people are not organized. They don't want to do the daily paperwork. They don't want to discipline themselves to list all the things that must happen daily, weekly, or monthly to achieve certain goals. But it's all part of the mix. There are certain things you must do every day to be successful. And you must make the time for them.

BOB FRARE: What else should a sales person pay attention to from a time management standpoint?

MARK FITZGERALD: The computer has changed today's selling environment dramatically. Sales people must set aside a part of each day to update themselves technologically—just to stay current. Most of the vendors and sales reps that contact me are totally electronic. They have a laptop with them. They're capable of producing a proposal within minutes. They've got voice mail and e-mail; they can communicate with their headquarters and get answers instantly. Sales people today must be up on all the latest technological advances in electronic communications and software and must continually update their computer skills to be effective. The computer properly used will shorten the selling cycle while increasing your success ratio. Contact management software, presentations, proposals, active up to date databases, forecasting, reports, faxing, and the Internet. Today's communication is called Field Sales Force Automation. Get a laptop computer and get connected.

BOB FRARE: Summarize for us what you suggest sales people need to pay close attention to to be successful as we move towards the next century.

MARK FITZGERALD: They must keep up on all the latest techniques and advances in selling, and share that knowledge with colleagues. They must have a system that moves them from account to account on a logical and progressive path. They need to continually update their technical knowledge and computer skills, and upgrade and become familiar with all the latest software. They must be self-motivated and have a support system to turn to on a constant and continual basis that spurs them on to be their own sales manager. They need effective sales training, like Partner Selling, that teaches them to be leaders, not followers, and which is constantly being reviewed and reinforced by management. Do all the right things consistently, and most importantly: GO SEE THE PEOPLE.

APPENDIX II

Automation: Changing the Ways People Sell

Technology pervades every aspect of our lives.

Its automated efficiencies have made day-to-day living easier and more carefree in many areas, and more challenging in others by fostering ongoing changes in the way we do things, changes that demand us to acquire additional expertise and master new skills all the time.

For example, while almost every household appliance these days is programmable in some way, requiring at least a degree of "computer savvy" on the part of the owner simply to operate it, personal computers themselves are not yet a fixture in every home. People still have a choice as to how high-tech they need and want to be at home.

But today's workplace is different. A "to be or not to be" high-tech choice no longer exists. PCs and their accompanying techno-aids and software have become *essential tools* in the running of every business and the performance of virtually every job. This includes such a "people job" as sales, where technology is assuming an increasingly important role in how sales people go about selling and serving clients to achieve win-win partnering relationships.

Companies whose sales people don't understand, deal with, or make an effort to use and master the latest automated systems and software available for everything from tracking and following up on leads to time management will get buried under an avalanche of ever-stiffer competition from those who do.

To shed some light on this critical topic, and to provide Partner Sellers with some valuable tips, I called on Joe Graziano, an expert in the field who has been helping companies use automated systems and software to cut debt, increase sales, and grow profits for more than fifteen years.

Joe began his career as an accountant, then moved into the computer sales field in the early 1980s when he recognized the need to help companies automate their financial systems operations to achieve a competitive edge.

To grow his own business, Joe developed a contact management software program that would help him keep better track of his mounting leads, prospects, and customers, since no such program yet existed on the market to facilitate this increasingly demanding aspect of the sales process.

When one of his clients expressed interest in the program, Joe, ever on the prowl for new opportunities, decided to sell the program plus the training to go with it. The venture took off.

As the contact management field matured and more advanced programs developed by others began to appear on the market, Joe moved into selling their software products to clients, and providing the required training as well.

Today, Joe's clients range from Fortune 500 companies to small and medium-sized ones with whom he consults on a wide range of technology issues confronting sales people, from sales automation systems and training to high-traffic Web site hosting. (If you'd like to contact Joe directly for more technology information, you may reach him at his Web site: www.joegraziano.com or call him at 973-831-0959.)

BOB FRARE: A computer is a basic necessity in business these days. What are the advantages/disadvantages of a laptop versus desktop computer to the sales professional?

JOE GRAZIANO: The obvious advantage is that a laptop is portable. You can tote it with you wherever you go. This gives you immediate access to client/prospect data at all times, allows you to receive and respond to important e-mail messages no matter where you are, and provides you with on-the-spot word processing capability to generate quotes and proposals so that clients/prospects don't have to wait for you to get back to them, and you can strike while the iron is hot. All the information about a client/prospect (name, address, phone number, e-mail address, Web site address, etc.) is in one easy-to-find place that is always at the sales person's fingertips. The sales person can keep better track of appointments (when, where, who, follow-up steps to be taken, you name it) and perform more effectively, on the road or anywhere.

BOB FRARE: So, whether it's a desktop or laptop, the computer can be used not only for database purposes but as a powerful pre- and post-planning and self-organizing tool as well.

JOE GRAZIANO: It *should* be used that way.

BOB FRARE: What's the downside to a laptop?

JOE GRAZIANO: The main one is cost. Most companies can't afford to provide their sales people with them—yet—because the average price of a laptop today is around $2,000. And as virtually every sales person already has a desktop or access to one at the office, some companies can't see going to the extra expense, especially since laptops, being so portable, can be lost or stolen very easily.

BOB FRARE: Are there any less expensive options available that offer some of the same advantages?

JOE GRAZIANO: Yes. There's the PDA, or Personal Digital Assistant. Some examples are the "Palm Pilot" and the "Nino." Virtually every electronics company manufactures a PDA. It's basically a small electronic device that fits in a shirt pocket, purse, or briefcase and can be easily carried, which allows you to transfer data collected on the road to your desktop PC and update client/prospect or record-keeping files automatically. Important notes to yourself don't get lost, and there is no duplication of information. Some PDAs even allow you to attach a modem to them so that you can send and receive e-mail messages while traveling. The average price is around $300. So, for slightly more than 10 percent of the cost of a laptop, companies can outfit all their sales people with these very useful tools much more affordably.

BOB FRARE: Let's move into the communications technology area. What are some of the best tools available for helping sales people improve response time with clients and prospects?

JOE GRAZIANO: Pagers and cell phones are at the top of the list. Pagers are a great tool for improving communications because clients and prospects can be given a number where they can reach you any time of the day or night to return their calls. Pagers are inexpensive to buy and use. Companies can provide them to their sales people quite economically. And with the advent of the alphanumeric pager and now the two-way pager, sales people can actually respond to other pagers, such as the customer's, from their own pagers, which is even more cost-effective.

BOB FRARE: What about cell phones?

JOR GRAZIANO: When they first came out, practically every company was supplying sales people with them. But the per-minute costs of the calls proved so prohibitive that many companies took the phones away, upsetting their sales people, who had found these tools very useful for conducting business. But in the last six months or so, AT&T, Bell Atlantic, and others have started offering a flat rate with no roaming or long distance charges for cell phone use, and many companies are letting their sales people have cell phones again. Most cell phone rates now are around ten to fourteen cents a minute for up to ten hours of usage a month.

BOB FRARE: Which competes quite favorably with land phone rates.

JOE GRAZIANO: Right. So, some of my clients are saying to their sales people, "We will pay $100 a month of your cell phone bill, you pay whatever is over that" on the assumption that the overage will be personal calls. This is more equitable, companies can now budget for the expense, which is no longer so open-ended, with the result being that they can make cell phones available to more and more of their people. Furthermore, cell phones themselves have become better. Today's digital cell phones offer alphanumeric paging with text messaging. This not only allows clients and prospects to page you and leave you their number, but to send you an e-mail about why they're calling.

BOB FRARE: In a nutshell, pagers and cell phones enable sales people to be more proactive.

JOE GRAZIANO: And not hamstring themselves from being proactive simply because they're en route someplace. They can be in contact with more people, more consistently, and, as a result, make more sales.

BOB FRARE: We've talked about the value of the computer and communications equipment as sales tools, now let's turn to one of the most critical aspects of the selling process, contact management. What is contact manager software?

JOE GRAZIANO: If a computer is your prime warehouse for storing information, the contact manager is your prime vehicle for getting and retrieving that information from the warehouse most efficiently. Its power is that it gives you the ability to place all, and I mean *all*, your information about a client or prospect in that one centralized location so that it is easily accessible to everyone. For example, let's say a sales person is charged with prospecting for *new business* with an existing customer, ABC Company. Bill, the sales person's prospect at ABC Company, calls for some information or material needed to push the sale forward, but the sales person is out of the office on another sales call. Because ABC Company is already a client, the customer service rep in the sales person's office can log onto the sales person's contact manager, record the nature of Bill's request, send the needed information or material out, note the action taken, and flag the sales person to follow up, all without the sales person's involvement, or even speaking to the sales person, yet ensuring that no important beat is missed.

BOB FRARE: In other words it frees sales people up to make the best use of their time.

JOE GRAZIANO: Exactly! It's also a very efficient tool for keeping sales managers in the loop so they can help their people more effectively without putting sales people to a lot of extra work that eats up valuable time.

BOB FRARE: How does it do that?

JOE GRAZIANO: In much the same way. One of the biggest gripes sales people have is paperwork, especially *additional* paperwork, such as making out call reports for sales managers *on top of* the sales activity reports they routinely input for themselves on a daily basis as an essential part of their job. What typically happens is that they wait until the end of the week to make out all these call reports at once, and the result ("Went to see so and so, dropped off samples.") is a meaningless exercise for all concerned. With contact manager software, there is zero extra work. The sales person inputs his or her daily sales activity report, and through the company's computer network, the sales manager can pull that report up on the screen on a daily basis as well, view what calls the person has made, what transpired, and determine what help the sales person may or may not need to push the sale forward without either party having to go to a lot of extra, time-consuming, and unnecessary work.

BOB FRARE: What is the opportunity management component of contact management software?

JOE GRAZIANO: Sales people don't just deal with one person, the decision-maker, and make a sale. To make the sale, they must deal with many different people within an organization who influence the decision-maker. Therefore, they have to know who these people are, the nature of the influence, and be able to target-market each of these people differently in order to have a positive impact on all the important players in the buying scenario. The opportunity management component allows sales people to input this type of information, and, most important, track it—so they can closely monitor all the various byways they must navigate to turn the opportunity into a sale. Contact management software gives them this vital capability.

BOB FRARE: What are some of the best contact manager software products available?

JOE GRAZIANO: The top brands are ACT, Gold Mine, Maximizer, Sales Logic, Smart Sales, and Telemagic. Those are the ones I recommend most strongly to my clients.

BOB FRARE: The Internet is becoming an exceedingly powerful sales tool.

JOE GRAZIANO: Yes. It's inexpensive too. Companies can get a Web site up and running, learn how to host and update it themselves or pay an outside consulting firm to handle that for them, for under $1,000 a year. Traditionally, companies have spent millions of dollars producing expensive brochures and all kinds of other sales literature for customers and prospects, which typically go unread, are thrown away, or lost. Now they can post all the information customers and prospects need and want about them and their products on their Web site, save those millions, and reach a greater number of people at the same time. Customers and prospects can access the promoted Web site address at their convenience, read up at their leisure, and the information they're provided is *always current*. Sales people don't have to lug around a lot of material that was probably outdated the minute it came off the presses, may be of little use to the customer or prospect as a take-way in its present form, and thus not a great selling tool.

BOB FRARE: What is an Intranet?

JOE GRAZIANO: An Intranet is a closed Internet site for private, intracompany use only. Outsiders, namely non-company personnel, cannot dial into it. Using a password, sales people can log on and have complete access quickly to whatever vital information the company wants them to have—current price lists, competitive information, and so on—that is not for public consumption. Sales managers can also use it to get that type of information to their people faster, more cheaply, and more securely than by phone or fax. The cost of an Intranet is about $20 a month, payable to the company's Internet provider, and e-mail service that comes with it is free. Web sites, the Internet, and Intranets are musts for companies these days.

BOB FRARE: As is all the other automation technology you've mentioned.

JOE GRAZIANO: Absolutely. Companies that don't avail themselves of these tools, and sales people who don't make use of and master them, are perceived by customers and prospects as too old-fashioned, too old-line, too unresponsive, too inconvenient, and not up to twenty-first century speed. That kind of perception is not exactly conducive to their wanting to do business with you.

APPENDIX III

Partner Selling Presentation Skills

Sales people are often called upon to present products or services before a group of clients and are judged as professionals by their performance. Therefore, the ability to speak effectively and hold an audience's attention is important to develop. And yet many sales people either ignore or fail to grasp even the most fundamental presentation skills.

There are a number of good courses available to help sales people enhance these all-important skills.

One of the best is the Dale Carnegie course *Effective Speaking in Human Relations,* an outstanding step-by-step program for helping people in any profession develop the confidence they need to effectively present themselves to others. The organization Toastmasters is another useful resource; it gives people the opportunity to practice and sharpen their presentation skills by speaking before live audiences.

Here are some other tips worth considering to make your next presentation before a group as dynamic as possible.

Understand Your Purpose

Before addressing the group, be sure you know what you intend to achieve.

Is your purpose to inform, entertain, sell, and persuade, or to initiate action, seek involvement, train, or teach? Or a combination of all these?

Create the Proper Logistics

Whenever I give a presentation, I make sure to find out beforehand the environment of the room I will be speaking in, the size of the group I will be speaking to, what will precede my talk, and what will follow it. In other words, I want as clear a picture as possible of the situation I'm walking into so I can make whatever adjustments in my setup I deem necessary.

I try to get into the room ahead of time to set up, but if that's not possible, I ask for a 5 to 10 minute break before my presentation to make those adjustments. This is very important because I want the way the room is set up to be well-suited to my style of speaking so I can be as relaxed and comfortable as possible.

Act Naturally

If you are too rigid and try to plan out your gestures, it will backfire on you—you may come across as insincere.

Strive to speak conversationally and let your body language flow naturally.

Some people are more animated than others. Be yourself. Whatever is natural is what will work best for you.

Use Visual Aids

Visual aids stimulate audience interest and involvement.

For small groups, I recommend a flip chart. For larger groups (twenty-five participants or more), I suggest using overhead transparencies.

If you use overheads, don't make your audience strain to read; put no more information on a single transparency than you would on a T-shirt, and avoid 8½ x 11 typewritten sheets.

For very large groups, slide and multi-media presentations can be very effective. PowerPoint software in combination with an LCD display is excellent for this.

Whatever visual aids you use, make sure they are large enough to be seen by the *entire* audience and that you do not compete with them. By that I mean, don't get in the way of them. On the other hand, don't hide behind them, either.

View the Presentation as an Opportunity for Self-Development

According to a study I read recently, 18 percent of those surveyed said their greatest fear was having to speak before a group. Their only greater fear was death (42 percent).

Overcoming fear of death is a one-time-only proposition. But in public speaking, the more you do it, the less fearful you will be of it, because the better you will get at it. This is why I encourage you to view every public speaking experience not with dread but as an opportunity for personal and professional growth—a way to move to the next level by improving your presentation skills.

The surest way to ease your fear of speaking and presenting is to concentrate on the message you are trying to communicate. If you are sure of your message—and believe in it—this will show. You will feel comfortable and confident, key ingredients in helping to dissipate whatever public speaking fears you may have.

Sell Yourself

Before the audience will buy the message, it must first buy the messenger.

If you can meet with the audience ahead of time, introduce yourself and get the group to know you a little bit before you start speaking; you will become a person to the audience, not just a talking head. And the audience will be warmer and more receptive to you and your message.

If you can't meet with the audience beforehand, supply the person who will be formally introducing you with a written introduction that imparts the same information and feelings about you.

Write the introduction yourself so you are sure it says *exactly* what you want it to say. The person introducing you will not be insulted. On the contrary, he or she will be grateful for being spared the work. And the introduction will be much more effective in selling you, the messenger.

Capture the Audience's Interest

Sweep the audience in and get it involved quickly.

Get up there, launch right into your presentation, and keep things moving!

The worst presenters are those who get off to a slow start or allow themselves to get bogged down, diluting audience interest.

To keep things flowing, make brief notes to organize your thoughts and help you stay on track. Never, *never* read your notes to the audience. Remember that you're making a presentation, not giving a speech. Maintain eye contact and strive for a conversational tone.

Don't Compete with Your Handouts

If you intend to hand out materials on the product or service you're presenting for the audience to keep and refer to, do it after you make your presentation not before.

Don't leave handouts on people's chairs for them to pick up as they arrive, or they will probably read them while you're talking. You will find yourself competing with your own handouts for the audience's attention throughout your presentation.

Use Humor Carefully

It is not imperative to use humor to be an effective presenter, but it helps a great deal. However, if you are not a funny person privately, you will not be a funny person publicly. Your efforts will likely come across as forced, or strained, and go over like the proverbial lead balloon.

I always practice any humorous elements I intend to use in my presentation. I rehearse before others so that when I go before my actual audience I am reasonably sure they will work.

When using humor, be careful not to ridicule any political or ethnic groups, or to criticize people. Try to make yourself the butt of the joke or humorous anecdote you are relating. Self-deprecating humor is always best in presentation situations.

Prepare an Ending to Your Presentation

It's surprising how many presenters leave their audiences hanging. They just stop talking, leaving the audience members to wonder if the presentation is over.

Concluding your presentation means just that. It requires coming up with an ending to your talk that wraps things up on a clear and crisp note that leaves no doubt in the audience's mind you are finished.

Establish Ahead of Time How You Are Going to Handle Q&A

You can either ask people to raise their hands during your presentation if they have questions and respond to them then, or ask the audience to hold its questions until after you have concluded your presentation. Either approach works well. Just decide which one it will be, tell the audience, and stick to it.

Occasionally it is necessary to break the ice by planting some questions beforehand. This is not duplicity but rather an important presentation skill designed to get questions flowing.

If you think such action may be required, and is appropriate, write a few questions down on a 3 X 5 card and arrange to have someone in the audience bring them up at the proper time. Be clear in your instructions: "When I say this, ask that question."

Keep the Q&A under Control

Don't let one member of the audience dominate the questioning.

Don't engage in a private conversation. When you respond to a question, do so to the entire audience, not just the person who asked it.

Don't let the Q&A drag on in periodic silence. Decide when it's over. If someone comes up with a question after that, say you will be happy to meet privately afterwards.

When it's over, it's over!

APPENDIX IV

Networking

Mastery of the art and skill of networking can have a tremendous impact on a sales person's career.

By expanding business contacts and making connections with the right people, networking enables you to grow your sphere of influence. The larger that sphere grows, the more opportunities present themselves for entering into win-win Partner Selling relationships.

Donna Fisher has written a great deal about this important art and skill in her books *Power Networking* and *People Power*. Here are some solid ideas Donna and I recommend to boost your skills in this area the next time a potential networking situation arises.

Recommended Reading on Nutrition and Fitness

As I mentioned in Chapter Six, proper nutrition and fitness are important though often neglected elements in keeping your energy level up and projecting thc image you wish to project to your clients. They also help to reduce daily stress and the negative impact that can have on job performance.

For further reading on nutrition and fitness, I recommend the following books:

Dr. Berger's Immunc Power Diet, Stuart M. Berger, M.D., New American Library, 1985.

Fit for Life, Harvey and Marilyn Diamond, Warner Books, 1985.

How to Be Your Own Nutritionist, Stuart M. Berger, M.D., Avon, 1988.

Let's Eat Right to Keep Fit, Adelle Davis, Signet, 1970.

Real Exercise for Real People, Peter Francis, Ph.D. and Lorna Francis Ph.D., Pummer Publishing, 1996.

Smart Exercise, Covert Bailey, Houghton Mifflin, 1994.

T-Factor 2000 Diet, The, Martin Katahn, Ph.D. and Jamie Pope, M.S., R.D., W.W. Norton & Company, 1995.

GLOSSARY

ACT!—Contact management software for managing schedules and client follow-up activities.

approach—The beginning of the sales process, where trust and rapport is established with the client or prospect and sales people sell themselves.

benefit—What the product or service will do for the client/prospect.

buying signals—Indicators given off by clients and prospects that show where they are in the buying process.

canned selling—Method generally used in telemarketing sales to "product dump" prospects from a script read over the phone.

client—Individual viewed by the sales person as having the potential for a long-term relationship and ongoing sales.

closing—Getting the client/prospect to make a commitment and move to the appropriate next step in the sales process.

commoditization—The process of products and services becoming widely available and equal and thus purchased solely on the basis of price.

customer—Individual viewed by the sales person as having the potential for a one-time-only transaction type of sale.

drive to succeed—The desire to achieve results or a goal and the persistence to do so.

empathy—The ability to understand and be sensitive to the client's needs, moods, and actions.

entering into relationship—The stage in the selling process when the client or prospect is moved forward to make a commitment, establishing a foundation for a long-term, mutually profitable buyer-seller union.

external customer—The client or prospect outside the sales person's company who is being serviced.

feature(s)—The indisputable fact(s) about what the product or service is.

goal—Sales expectation, generally established by oneself.

Gold Mine—Contact management software for managing schedules and client follow-up activities.

hard-sell tactics—Outdated traditional selling techniques used to muscle and manipulate the client into buying.

high-risk questions—Trial close questions asked of a client or prospect specifically to elicit a response that will lead to a decision.

internal customer—Any member of the sales person's support team who interfaces with the external customer.

jargon—Language germane to a particular business, industry, or field.

Low-risk questions—Relaxed and easygoing trial close questions that ask the client/prospect for a general opinion, not a decision.

maximizer—Contact management software for managing schedules and client follow-up activities.

members—Those clients or customers serviced by an organization.

motivational support—Books, audiotapes, videos, sales training courses, and ongoing general support provided to sales people to stimulate professional growth and enhance performance.

negative responses—Objections from clients to probing trial close questions, telling sales people they are off the track.

negotiate—To find out what's troubling or stopping the client/prospect from moving forward and closing the sale.

partnering—Understanding the client's problems and addressing them to achieve a win-win outcome.

patients—Those clients or customers serviced by doctors, hospitals, and health care organizations.

positive responses—Affirmative replies to probing questions that tell sales people they are on the right track with clients.

premature price questions—Questions raised by clients about price before value has been communicated or demonstrated.

pre-planning—Collecting as much relevant information on the client or prospect beforehand to facilitate handling almost any eventuality during the face-to-face presentation.

probing—Asking short *what, where, when, why, how,* and *who* questions designed to get clients and prospects to open up and reveal more information about their needs.

product dump—The overloading of product feature information on the client.

product knowledge—The essential information a sales person must have to be able to sell a particular product or service.

quota—Sales expectation, generally established by someone else.

reviewing needs—Identification of the client or prospect's needs, concerns, experiences, and desires to determine if there is a potential for a win-win outcome.

Sales Logic—Contact management software for managing schedules and client follow-up activities.

sales pitch—Traditional selling term emphasizing a lopsided "Lemme tell ya what I can do for you" approach.

sales pressure—Stress placed on the client by the sales person to move toward a decision.

sales skills—Demonstrable abilities a sales person must have to succeed.

selling attitude—Positive feelings a sales person must have about selling and helping clients to move forward with conviction, confidence, and determination.

selling system—Strategic, organized approach to the selling or buying process marked by a beginning, middle, and end.

selling yourself—Getting clients/prospects to like you and have a high level of trust in you.

selling yourself first—The merging of the sales person's strong product belief with an equally strong belief that the product is the right solution to the client/prospect's problems.

Smart Sales—Contact management software for managing schedules and client follow-up activities.

supplier—The vendor or person doing the selling.

Telemagic—Contact management software for managing schedules and client follow-up activities.

testimonials—Third party endorsements of a product or service, verbal or written.

traditional selling—Hard line, manipulative selling tactics of the past that are resisted by clients.

transaction—One-time-only sale involving no relationship or ongoing sales goals.

translate value—To communicate how the product or service being offered will address the client's specific needs and achieve specific goals.

trial close questions—Questions asked by the sales person to find out where the client/prospect is in the buying process.

win-win—When the sales person and the client profit mutually from the relationship.

INDEX

Q

R

S

About the Author

Bob Frare has been in the training and development field for more than twenty years and a popular professional speaker on the subject since 1981. He was an award-winning sales person with three of the leading training organizations in the country before founding his own company. He has addressed more than 3,500 audiences and spoken to sales groups all across the United States and Canada. He enjoys a ten handicap in golf and has a teenage daughter, Jaime. You can contact Bob at 1-877-298-1904, or via the Internet at www.partnerselling.com.